LaGrange Public Library
LaGrange, Illinois  60525
708-352-0576

# IRISH
# WEDDING
# TRADITIONS

*The author's paternal grandmother,*
*Mrs. John Francis McMahon, on her wedding day, June 16, 1920.*

# IRISH

*Using Your Irish*

# WEDDING

*Heritage to Create the*

# TRADITIONS

*Perfect Wedding*

## Shannon McMahon Lichte

*Illustrations by Patricia Brentano*

HYPERION
*New York*

*To my husband, Richard Lichte,*

whose love and patience

inspired these pages.

'Tis all for thee . . .

*Acknowledgments*

I WOULD LIKE TO THANK my agent, Claudia Cross,
for her belief in this project and her amazing support through
the process; editor Maureen O'Brien for all her hard work
and inspiration; Richard Oriolo for his beautiful book
design; Patricia Brentano for the lovely drawings; James
Hirsch for his website design; Sara Kennedy for her
embroidery designs for the end pages; Adam Weinberg for
his gardening tips; Lady Ardane for permission to reprint
her handfasting ritual, Cait Finnegan for permission to use
her poetry in this book, Morgan Llywelyn for the use of her

Celtic wedding vows, and Sr. Mary Ruth Murphy for permission to use her blessing.

Thanks to the following people who shared with me their knowledge of things Irish: Dermot McEvoy, Malachy McCourt, Peter Quinn, my favorite Cork man Con Horgan (your Irish heart is the biggest there is), Tara Fay, Patrick Coleman at the Traditional Irish Bakery, Joannie Langbroek and Rosanna Mulligan at Cakes & Co., and Eileen Reilly for her pictures of strawboys.

Special thanks to all my friends and family who have lived this book with me every day for three years, including Sara Margaret Beall; Karla, Todd, David, and Dossy McMahon; Carmelyn McMahon Johnson; Amy Brentano, the best example I know of artistry and grace under pressure; Mike Sheresky for believing in one of my cockamamie schemes; GADA West, Red Earth East, and all of those dear to me who are associated with these great institutions; the Shawn Mackey family; Heidi Anderson, Ellen Adamson, Cameron Watson, and Allison Janney for daily emotional support and occasional whip-cracking.

LIKE MANY PEOPLE OF IRISH DESCENT, I have spent my life wondering about my ancestors, their personal histories, and what makes me "Irish." I feel an immediate attachment and a sense of belonging when I hear a bit of Irish music or read a phrase of Irish poetry. I look at the old photographs of my grandparents and their parents before them and wonder about their struggles to create a home and family here in America.

The morning of my thirty-fifth birthday was the first time I ever touched Irish soil. My lifelong dream to visit the country of my ancestors had finally come true. With great anticipation, I looked down on my namesake, the River Shannon, from the small window of the airplane. "Home." That's the feeling that came over me. Over the next few weeks of that first trip, I was struck time and again by the wonderful feeling of being home.

A few months later, when I fell in love with my husband, it seemed only appropriate to include my Irish heritage, for which I had such a strong affinity, as part of our wedding day. I began searching for anything I could find about Irish weddings. I was quite surprised to learn that there was very little published about Ireland's wedding customs and traditions here in America. During our honeymoon in Ireland, I began collecting some of the customs, traditions, and superstitions that appear in this book. I am greatly indebted to the many Irish scholars, including Kevin Danaher, Linda May Ballard, and Maria Buckley, who have recorded Ireland's wedding traditions from the past.

What I have tried to do in much of *Irish Wedding Traditions* is to update many of the oldest Irish wedding customs so that they can be used in a contemporary wedding. I have also included many of the Irish wedding practices that are currently popular in Ireland so that a couple may have many different Irish traditions to choose from when planning their wedding.

When people get married, they will often reflect about their heritage as they make plans for creating a new branch of the family tree. I hope a newly engaged couple will find this book a helpful way to honor their family and, most importantly, each other.

# Contents

Whatever joys await the blest above,
no bliss below like happy wedded love.

WILLIAM ALLINGHAM (b. 1824)

*Donegal*

# IRISH
# WEDDING
# TRADITIONS

# Chapter One

# WOOING TO PROPOSAL

Irish Customs for Courtship

THE IRISH, BEING A ROMANTIC, emotional, and superstitious people, have many different customs that relate to the sacrament of marriage. Before discussing courtship and marriage customs, we must first look back at the history of Irish betrothal.

The earliest mention of marriage came from Gaelic tribes who roamed the countryside of ancient Ireland. Patrick Powers, in his book *Sex and Marriage in Ancient Ireland*, explains that marriage fell under the brehon laws, which formed Ireland's legal system before the Norman conquests in the twelfth century. The brehon laws were first recorded in the fifth century, with the introduction of Christianity to Ireland, but are believed to have existed long before that.

Under brehon law, the Gaelic word for marriage, *lanamnus*, can be translated as "a social connection for the purpose of procreation." The brehon laws determined who could contract a proper marriage and the obligations of a married couple, including how their children would be raised. The brehon laws also defined the dowry for a bride and groom. *Tinnscra* was a dowry or bride-price that was paid to the father of the bride if the bride was taken away from her tribe, or *tuath*. Under brehon laws the marriage of a man and woman was a marriage of equals, with the woman having equal rights when it came to both children and property.

As Christianity became more widespread in Ireland, marriage began to be governed by the Church. The Irish would often marry at home until the late eighteenth century, when it was deemed improper and invalid to marry anywhere but within the Church.

Arranged marriages were common in Ireland during the sixteenth and seventeenth centuries and were even more common in rural areas well into the twentieth century. These marriages were often arranged by a local matchmaker.

Matchmaking will be discussed in this chapter, along with superstitions about when to marry and divination customs, which foretold who one would marry. These were all practices common among the rural Irish. Engagement practices will also be mentioned in this chapter, including a discussion of engagement and wedding rings favored by the Irish.

## *Divination*

DIVINATION IS THE mystical practice of foretelling the future. In rural Ireland, peasants had many different rituals for divination. One favorite use was to discover when and if you were destined for marriage as well as the identity of the person you were destined to marry.

The popularity of divination among young people may have been related to the fact that marriages were often arranged affairs. This was especially true in the farming communities where most young people were allowed little choice of a marriage partner. The act of divination may have been a countermeasure to the lack of personal control in the matter.

Here are some examples of Irish divination rituals:

- A young woman would pick a handful of daisies with one hand. The number of daisies she held foretold the number of years that remained before she married.

- A wedding ring was placed in a bowl of the potato dish Colcannon, and the person who was served up the ring in his or her portion would be the next to marry.

+ Young girls would go to haystacks at midnight and pull out a piece of hay. It was believed if the straw was straight and unbroken, the future husband would be gentle and kind. If the straw was knotted or bent and twisted, he would be an angry old man.

+ Four variously filled dishes and one empty dish are placed in front of a blindfolded young man or woman. If the person chose the empty dish, they would never marry. If they chose the dish with water, they would emigrate overseas. If they chose the dish with earth, it meant an early grave. The dish filled with salt was a sign that a person would shed tears and have much heartache in life. If they chose the dish with a wedding ring, they were sure to marry.

+ It was believed that sleeping with a piece of wedding cake under a pillow would induce a young woman to dream of her future husband.

+ The Irish traveling community, in the past known as tinkers, have many superstitions for identifying a future spouse. If young travelers wanted to know the name of a future husband or wife, they would throw an apple peel over their left shoulder. It was said the peel would fall into the shape of their future spouse's first initial.

# The Irish Matchmaker

*You get two lonely people together for a bit of nice conversation and it's like they've known each other all of their lives.* —THE MATCHMAKER

BY THE EIGHTEENTH and nineteenth centuries, as in many other countries of the world, most all of Ireland was engaged in the custom of arranged or "made" marriages, especially in the more rural parts of the country. Many marriages were arranged by a local matchmaker, who was the go-between for families interested in marrying their children. A dowry was a very important part of the match. Families would negotiate for land and livestock, making sure that each party brought an equal amount to the table. In most cases the young people involved had already begun to carry on a courtship.

Matchmaking still exists in Ireland today, especially on the west coast. Every September the tiny town of Lisdoon-varna in County Clare is overrun with eligible men and women who come for its annual matchmaking festival. In the past, the festival was always held right after the harvest, so that farmers could get a little relaxation—and a new wife, if needed. Today the matchmaking festival seems to be an excellent excuse for merrymaking, with much music and singing in pubs.

Likewise, up in Knock, County Mayo, Rev. Michael Keane runs the Knock Marriage Bureau, which has 745 marriages to its credit as of the year 2000. Interested parties write the Reverend Keane and he responds with a question-naire, so he can make a proper introduction from his wide base of eligible men and women. There is also a father/daughter team of matchmakers in County Clare who set up introductions as well as informal matchmaking on the Aran Islands and on the Dingle Peninsula. Matchmaking is still quite alive in modern-day Ireland.

If you and your intended were introduced by a friend or family member, it would be a lovely idea to honor your "matchmaker" at the wedding with a special acknowledg-ment. Perhaps you can offer up a toast at the reception, giv-ing heartfelt thanks to this most important person who brought you together. Be sure to mention in the toast that this friend followed in the traditions of a real Irish match-maker.

# An Irish Proposal

THERE IS A tradition in rural Ireland that can be adapted for a modern wedding proposal. Padraic O'Farrell speaks of this tradition in his book *Superstitions of the Irish Country People*. A groom takes his bride to a stream, mill, or tree, all symbols of a lasting endurance. He then presents his bride with newly churned butter, which was a luxury in rural Ireland, especially during the famine years. The butter may have symbolized the abundance and wealth a man hoped for in his marriage. As the groom presented the fresh butter to his bride, he recited the following prayer:

*Oh woman, loved by me, mayest thou*
*give me thy heart, thy soul and body.*

This would be a beautiful custom to use for a marriage proposal. A man (or woman for that matter!) could take his beloved to a stream near a tree for a picnic. A covered butter dish can hide the engagement ring to honor this part of the tradition. The words of the prayer can be written down and tucked inside the butter dish with the ring, although speaking the words out loud would be a most romantic and unforgettable gesture.

# When to Marry

THE IRISH HAVE always had very strong beliefs about the time of year and even the day one should marry. Here are some beliefs that have been passed down through the centuries. In ancient Celtic times, couples would often marry during one of the Irish fire festivals.

*Beltaine*—This festival, commencing around the first of May, is a celebration of the return of life and fertility. Beltaine marks the beginning of summer in the old Irish calendar. The word *beltaine* is thought to mean brilliant or new fire. This spring fire festival was a time for the ceremonial matrimony between god and goddess in Celtic mythology, hence its popularity among betrothed mortals.

Bonfires were lit during the Beltaine festival, and the ancient Celts would dance around them. Couples who choose to marry at Beltaine and are having an outdoor reception can plan to light a bonfire in honor of the bright fire tradition.

The ancient Irish also practiced the custom of decorating the May bush. A bush, or small tree, would be decorated with brightly colored ribbons, with a ball made of brightly colored paper at the top. Friends of the bride and groom would present the tree or bush to a newly married couple, and all would dance around it. This is similar to the Maypole, which was popular in other Celtic countries, and either one would be a beautiful decorative touch to the wedding reception decor.

*Lughnassadh*—This festival in early August is a celebration of the first day of Celtic autumn and the beginning of the harvest. Lughnassadh attracted huge assemblies of Celtic people. Many Celtic historians believe that this was one of the most popular times for marriage.

Young men who hired themselves out to work the harvest would often end up wintering where they worked. Therefore, taking a wife would be beneficial, providing a companion for the long winter. Most commitments were made during festival time, as once the harvest began there would be little time for courtship.

A popular gathering place for Lughnassadh during the seventeenth century was Teltown, County Meath, which featured "Teltown marriages." These marriages were performed in a spot known as "marriage hollow." The lovers participating in the ceremony would often hold hands through a holed stone.

Because Lughnassadh takes place before the harvest, there would be a great deal of feasting, as people would eat up the last of their stored food. To honor the harvest, marrying at this time of year can include a reception resplendent with harvested local vegetables. The first wild berries can also be found at this time in Ireland, and berries can be used as a central part of the wedding feast. A berry-laden wedding cake would be in keeping with the spirit of Lughnassadh.

*Samhain*—A couple planning to marry in the fall may want to consider marrying around the late October–early November festival known as Samhain.

Samhain means November in the Irish language and is also thought to mean, more generally, summer's end or the beginning of the twilight period of winter. During this season the Celts would begin preparing for the long winter after culling the abundance of their harvest.

Using symbols of the harvest in the wedding decor is a creative way to celebrate Samhain. Shafts of wheat can be used as centerpieces at reception tables, along with harvested fruits and vegetables.

Storytelling by local bards started around this time each year, and in many chieftains' halls it was mandatory that a story be told every night during the winter months. This could be an entertaining custom to re-create. Asking friends and family to tell stories about the bride and groom will add a warm touch to a Samhain wedding.

*Imbolc*—This feast day celebrated around February 1 is considered the first day of spring in the Celtic calendar. The Celts celebrated the first stirring of the earth from its arctic sleep. Ceremonial fires were lit to celebrate the awakening of the earth and the new season to come. To get married during Imbolc is to celebrate the new life a bride and groom will share together.

As part of the Imbolc feast, fresh lamb would be served, the first fresh meat after a long winter. Lamb is still a very popular dish in Ireland and is often served at wedding receptions.

Another way to celebrate the Imbolc festival would be to give out seed packets as wedding favors, as a symbol of growth and the first day of spring. Shamrock seeds would be an appropriate choice, or you can give the seeds of a flower used in the bride's wedding bouquet.

Here are some other beliefs about when to marry, many of them rural customs from the nineteenth and early twentieth centuries.

At one time Shrove Tuesday, the last Tuesday before Lent, was considered the proper time to marry. Since Lent is a time of abstention from meat, eggs, milk, and alcohol, Shrove Tuesday would be the last day for feasting, the last time wedding guests could fully partake of wedding celebrations until Easter.

Among the rich foods served on Shrove Tuesday, pancakes were always a favorite because they used up all the eggs and dairy products left in the pantry. Many Irish still call the Tuesday before Lent "pancake day." If marrying at Shrovetide you may want to serve blinis, mini-pancakes topped with salmon caviar, as an hors d'oeuvre at the reception. This is an elegant way to modify the Shrovetide pancake tradition.

November was a favorite time for weddings in the ninth century. This was most likely true because the summer harvest was completed and the people had more food and wealth in the fall than at any other time of year.

November marriages were also popular in the early twentieth century. A rhyme heard on Clare Island, off the west coast of Ireland, states:

> November is said time to wed.
> The crops is made and no warmth in bed!

Lady Wilde, the mother of Oscar Wilde, collected hundreds of ancient cures, spells, and homespun proverbs from Irish peasants in the nineteenth century. In her book *Irish Cures, Mystic Charms and Superstitions*, Lady Wilde records a different sentiment about planning to marry in the fall. Some believed that "those who marry in autumn will die in spring."

There are other favorable days to marry, according to Irish tradition. Christmas and New Year's are considered lucky days to tie the knot, as is St. Patrick's Day. The last day of the old year is also thought to be especially lucky for weddings; it is thought that your last memories of the year you marry should be the happiest ones.

# Wedding Rings

WEDDING RINGS ARE a couple's public pledge of commitment. A ring on the fourth finger of the left hand expresses to the world that you love and are loved. It was once believed in Ireland that wedding rings were worn on the fourth finger of the left hand because the blood line or artery in this finger connected directly to the heart.

Wedding rings have been a part of marriage since the earliest days of civilization. The betrothal ritual involved the exchange of property between the groom-to-be and the bride's parents. This was an important part of the marriage contract because the bride's family was losing her to another lineage. The engagement or betrothal ring was partial payment for the bride and dates back to the ancient days when gold rings were circulated as currency.

Gold rings were so important in eighteenth-century Ireland that poor couples would rent rings for their ceremony. W. Tegy, in his book *The Knot Tied*, says, "it is believed unless the wedding ring be golden, the marriage lacks validity." Couples who could not afford a gold ring have been known to use the loop of the door key to their new home or to the church as a symbolic ring.

A ring, being an unbroken circle, is considered to be a symbol of perfection. It is perfect unity without beginning or end. The rings you choose will remain a constant reminder of the unity you pledge on your wedding day. Choosing a ring with an Irish history will be a daily reminder of your heritage, a tribute to your family, as well as a symbol of your enduring promise to each other. On the following pages are some ideas for rings that will honor your Irish heritage.

 *The Claddagh Ring*

*Love—Friendship—Loyalty*

THE CLADDAGH RING is perhaps the most popular and well-known symbol of love in Ireland. The ring's design is of two hands holding a heart that wears a crown. According to the Claddagh Ring Museum, at Thomas Dillon's jewelry store in Galway, the motif is explained in the phrase "Let Love and Friendship reign." The hands symbolize friendship, the heart love, and the crown loyalty.

The ring is named for a small fishing village outside Galway, and there are many folk legends about how the ring came into existence. One legend has it that Claddagh developed the ring to be worn by the fishermen and sailors as a means of identifying them in case they went overboard, were lost at sea, and washed ashore on strange soil.

Another version of the Claddagh ring's origin is the story of sixteenth-century Irish philanthropist Margaret Joyce. Margaret was left a fortune by her husband, a wealthy Spanish merchant. She used the money to build bridges from Galway to Sligo. It was said that she was rewarded for her good works and charity by an eagle, who swooped down one sunny afternoon as she was sitting by the shores of Galway Bay and dropped the original Claddagh ring into her lap.

The most romantic Claddagh legend is the story of another member of the Joyce clan, Richard Joyce. Joyce was captured by Algerian pirates on his way to the West Indies and forced into slavery working for a Moorish goldsmith. He became a master at his trade and handcrafted a ring for a woman back home whom he could not forget. In 1689, Joyce was released after William III came into power. He returned to Claddagh, where he found that the woman he loved had never married. He gave her the ring, and she used the Claddagh as a wedding band when they married. Joyce set up a goldsmith shop, and examples of his work, marked with an anchor signifying hope and the initials RJ, still exist.

The Claddagh ring is considered a fede, or faith ring, which was very popular in the Middle Ages. The ring has become popular outside of Ireland since the nineteenth century, leaving Ireland on the hands of the many Irish men and women who emigrated during the Great Famine. These rings were kept as heirlooms with great pride and were passed from mother to daughter to use as wedding bands.

Today a couple can choose many different variations of the Claddagh ring, including rings inlaid with precious stones such as diamonds and emeralds.

As a wedding band, the ring is usually worn on the fourth finger of the left hand, with the point of the heart worn inward. This indicates to the world that the wearer is married; the heart being happily taken.

 # The Celtic Wedding Ring

RINGS WITH DESIGNS inspired by Celtic art have become very popular with Irish couples in recent years. Celtic civilization had many artisans who incorporated their designs into their daily lives by decorating their houses of worship, garments, tools of war, and burial tombs.

History has not recorded exactly what the different Celtic designs mean, but many designs have been given meanings over the centuries by those who continue to use them.

Celtic wedding rings most often use what has come to be known as the Celtic love knot. This is a pattern that is created by using continuous unending lines. The intertwined designs symbolize eternity, unity, and fidelity. The wearing of these rings signifies that a bond has been formed. The lines of the Celtic love knot are forever intertwined, as two separate lives become one.

Ancient Celtic artists also used animal designs to show how Celtic lives were interwoven with nature. One of the most popular animals used for Celtic wedding rings is the heron, because herons mate for life.

Couples who choose a wedding ring with a Celtic design will be honoring one of the most ancient aspects of their Irish heritage.

## The Emerald Ring

*"The Wearing of the Green . . ."*

MANY MODERN-DAY Irish American couples have opted to use emeralds in their engagement rings and wedding bands instead of the traditional diamond. With pride, an emerald acknowledges that the couple are descendants of the "Emerald Isle."

An emerald's rich green color, the color of spring, was

prized by ancient civilizations who believed the gemstone represented love and rebirth. According to the International Colored Gemstone Association, emeralds are said to quicken the intelligence as well as the heart. Legend also has it that an emerald bestows upon its owner the gift of eloquence.

Emeralds range in color from deep grass green to a light yellowish green. The more vivid the green, the more valuable the emerald. Emeralds are mined in South America, Egypt, Brazil, and Russia. They are rare and expensive to mine. Top-quality emeralds can run thousands of dollars per carat. It is also possible to find the less expensive beryle, a man-made stone in an emerald green color, which has become very popular, in many jewelry stores.

When choosing an emerald, couples should remember that it is considered a most magical stone by forest spirits and Irish fairies. Great care must be taken when a bride wears an emerald, as she could be spirited away by the little people!

# The Gimmal Ring

A GIMMAL RING is a ring that joins with another to complete an image. In medieval times these interlocking rings, often in three parts, were used as a promise of betrothal.

*Tying the Knot*, a booklet published by the Ulster Folk and Transport Museum, states that at the time of the marriage contract, "one each of the three parts of the ring was kept respectively by the girl, her suitor, and the priest. The three parts were reunited at the marriage ceremony and were worn by the bride as her wedding ring."

Gimmal rings often have a look similar to the Irish Claddagh ring. Usually, the ring's design is two hands that surround and cover a hidden heart or hearts. Modern–day gimmal rings have been crafted as one unit, with the hands hinged. When opened, the hands expose the heart hidden underneath.

For something truly unusual, a gimmal ring might be worn as a wedding band to convey a couple's Irish heritage, instead of wearing the traditional Claddagh ring.

# THE CELTIC CROSS
# TO THE HERALDIC
# HARP

Incorporating the Customs and
Symbols of Ireland into
the Wedding Day

AS A COUPLE BEGINS TO plan their wedding day, the
first question that comes to mind about incorporating their
Irish heritage is: What represents Ireland?

Is it the leprechauns and shamrocks one associates with
St. Patrick's Day? Or is it the exquisite art and decorative
images from the eighth–century illuminated gospels, the
*Book of Kells*? Perhaps Ireland is defined by the stories of
Celtic kings who roamed the ancient Irish countryside or
the myths of fairies who still rule Ireland's underground
spirit world. Possibly it's the stories and pictures of Irish

ancestors that have inspired a couple to incorporate their heritage into their special day.

Ireland is all of these things. In this chapter, these images and historical traditions will be defined and ways to include Irish symbols and customs into all aspects of the wedding day will be suggested. These bits of Irish history can inspire a couple to add an Irish touch to their invitations, wedding attire, flowers, and even the decor for the ceremony and reception.

Along with visual ideas, this chapter will introduce wedding customs that were popular in Ireland during the nineteenth century, as well as some wedding conventions that are common in Ireland today. These symbols and historical anecdotes will encourage a couple to wholeheartedly embrace their Irish spirit.

There are many different images that come to mind when one thinks of Ireland. There are the national and cultural symbols of Ireland, as well as ancient Celtic symbols that decorate many religious and historical monuments throughout the country. There are also images that have been attributed historically to the different families of Ireland, known as "clans," in the Middle Ages.

Understanding the historical relevance and cultural significance of these Irish symbols will make it easier for a couple to choose the ones that will best represent them on their wedding day.

Couples can use these images to decorate their wedding invitations, which are usually the first indication to guests of the style and formality of the wedding. Invitations with an Irish design will set the tone for the wedding day to come.

A couple can also use Irish images when choosing the decor for the ceremony and the reception, and may even incorporate them into their wedding attire and wedding cake design.

# The Shamrock

*May your blessings outnumber the shamrocks you grow . . .*

NO SYMBOL IS more identified with Ireland than the tiny green plant, the shamrock. The word *shamrock* comes from the Irish word *seamrog*, meaning little clover.

It is common wisdom in Ireland that St. Patrick used the shamrock to explain the Holy Trinity. Holding up a shamrock, the saint explained to the curious Irish that the three leaves represent the Father, Son, and Holy Spirit, but the one stalk represented one God. Lady Wilde mentions that the shamrock "enlightens the brain and makes one see and know the truth."

In 1620 Sir John Melton wrote: "If a man walking the fields find any four-leafed grass, he shall, in a small while after, find some good thing." The four-leaf clover has since been universally accepted as a symbol of good luck, and according to legend, Eve carried a four-leaf clover when banished from the Garden of Eden.

According to Irish legend, each leaf of the lucky four-leaf clover has a special meaning, all of which are quite appropriate to symbolize the wedding day . . .

*One leaf for Hope, the second for Faith,*
*the third for Love, and the fourth for Luck!*

## Growing Shamrocks

LIVE SHAMROCKS CAN be a part of every couple's wedding day. Shamrocks will not last long when cut, so the best option is to grow them in individual containers so they can be put on tables at the wedding reception. Small clay pots painted to match the rest of the wedding decor will add a festive touch and lots of luck for the marriage.

The clover known as *Oxalis acetosella* is the easiest to grow from seeds. The seeds can be purchased at garden centers or from seed catalogs. Garden designer Adam Weinberg offers these tips on growing *Oxalis*.

1. Seeds should be placed in four-inch pots on moist soil and then very lightly covered with more soil, leaving two inches from the soil to the top of the pot.

2. Plastic should then be placed over the pots. The pots should be stored in a warm, shaded location until the seeds have germinated.

3. When the first leaves appear, remove the plastic and place the pots in a sunny location. Keep the soil moist.

4. When four or five clovers have appeared, you can fertilize the pots with an indoor fertilizer and continue fertilizing every two to three weeks.

5. Once the plants have established, thin out any that look unhealthy. It should take about six to eight weeks after germination for the *Oxalis* to be in healthy green abundance.

# The Heraldic Harp

IT MAY BE surprising to learn that the national symbol of Ireland is not the shamrock as many think, but the heraldic harp. The harp has been associated with Ireland for many centuries. Images of harps can be found carved on Irish stones that date back to the twelfth century.

In ancient Ireland, professional harpers were honored above all other musicians. Irish harpers often played before the high chiefs of Ireland. Sadly many of the old melodies and songs have been lost, as harp music was not written down, but was passed down from teacher to student.

The symbol of the harp is currently used by the government of Ireland on the seal of the president, as well as being used on the nation's coins. The model for the artistic representation of the heraldic harp is based on the fourteenth-century harp now preserved in the museum of the Trinity College, Dublin. Popularly known as the Brian Boru harp, this harp, which is the oldest surviving harp on Irish soil, was named after the eleventh-century king of Ireland.

Using the symbol of a heraldic harp in wedding decor adds an aristocratic touch, as well as being an elegant symbol of a couple's Irish nationalism.

# Celtic Art and Designs

IRELAND HAS A rich artistic history and the ancient Celts were one of the greatest contributors to this legacy. Celtic artwork dates back to 3000 B.C. and can still be seen on stone carvings throughout Ireland. The ancient burial mound, Newgrange, thought to be one of the oldest burial sites in Europe, has many Celtic decorative motifs, including numerous spiral designs. The spirals may represent the elements of earth, sky, and water, or possibly the sun.

Much of the current fascination with Celtic art can be attributed to the *Book of Kells*. This is an eighth-century manuscript that was created by monks of the Collum Cillae order.

The manuscript includes elaborate illustrations of the four gospels and has been called "the most beautiful book in the world." The manuscript can be viewed at Trinity College in Dublin.

The *Book of Kells* features many interlacing, unending patterns, as well as animal designs and triquetras, a three-pronged knot design believed to represent the Holy Trinity. The unbroken pattern in Celtic design is thought to represent a spiritual growth that is never ending, as well as enduring love.

Any of these Celtic-inspired designs would be a most appropriate choice for Irish wedding decorations.

## The Tricolor

A COLORFUL TOUCH can be added to the wedding decor by using Ireland's flag. The national flag of the Republic of Ireland is popularly known as the tricolor.

The flag is made up of three equal vertical stripes of color, in green, white, and orange. These colors represent Ireland's political landscape: green symbolizes the Catholics of Ireland, orange the Protestants, and white represents the hope of a lasting peace between them. Thomas Francis Meagher, a member of the Young Ireland Movement, introduced the tricolor in 1848, but it was not adopted as the national flag of Ireland until 1921, when Ireland gained its independence from Britain.

The colors of the tricolor were used with great fanfare at the Boston wedding of an Irish couple in the 1960s. The bride, being Irish Catholic, had her bridesmaids dressed in pale green dresses, while the groom, a proud Irish Protestant, dressed his groomsmen in tuxedos of a light coral color. The bride and groom then both wore white, sending out the message to both families that this would be a happy, peaceful union.

A more subtle way to include the tricolor is to decorate

the cars carrying the bride, groom, and wedding party with Irish flags. This will give the vehicles a grand, stately appearance as the flags wave in the wind, as well as represent the couple's heartfelt nationalism.

# The Celtic Cross

A LOVELY SYMBOL with both religious and cultural meaning for the Irish is the Celtic cross. These crosses, carved in stone, can be found all across Ireland, with the oldest one residing at the ancient Christian church of Clonmacnois in County Offaly.

The earliest crosses carved by Celtic craftsmen are thought to illustrate stories from the Bible, although some believe the oldest crosses predate Christianity and were carved to represent the claims and ambitions of Irish kings.

The ring enclosing the crux, which is a distinctive part of the Celtic cross, has many different interpretations. Mike Carson, an archaeologist who has studied Celtic crosses, is of the opinion that the ringed aspect of a Celtic cross symbolizes the seasonal equinoxes and solstices, or perhaps the four seasonal Celtic festivals: Beltaine, Lughnassadh, Samhain, and Imbolc.

Many Irish historians believe the ring has a connection with the sun. Cari Buzik, a Canadian artist who specializes in Celtic design, believes the four parts of the cross represent the four parts of man—the mind, body, soul, and heart.

## The Family Coat of Arms

A COUPLE MAY want to celebrate the joining of their families by choosing to use their coats of arms in their wedding decor.

Heraldry, the language of emblems, grew out of the military life of the Middle Ages. Knights in battle would wear jupons (a long vest) covering their chain-mail coats, and these would be decorated with their coat of arms so the combatants could be recognized in battle.

These emblems were assigned by chief heralds, usually appointed by the king in power. There has been a chief herald in Ireland since the 1500s, according to the Irish Heraldica Organization. It is common for the president of Ireland to receive a coat of arms toward the end of his or her term in office, which is then displayed on a shield hung on the grand staircase of Dublin Castle.

There are now thousands of names that have been given coats of arms in the world, and many Irish coats of arms have been passed down through the great clans of Ireland. Coats of arms can be used on wedding invitations or even embroidered on wedding attire for both the bride and groom.

# The Tara Brooch

THE CELTIC PEOPLE of ancient Ireland had a great love of decorative ornamentation. Many beautifully crafted gold and silver pieces have survived, including rings, bracelets, necklets, and ornamental brooches.

Perhaps the most famous of these ornamental pieces is the Tara Brooch. Brooches were worn by both men and women in ancient times to fasten garments, and persons of high standing wore brooches made of precious metals set with decorative gemstones. Although it is not known who originally wore the Tara Brooch, it is assumed, because of its valuable jewels, that it was worn by a person of high rank in a Celtic clan.

The Tara Brooch has been widely reproduced in Ireland as a piece of jewelry, as well as being depicted in many drawings and paintings. It has also become popular to represent the Tara Brooch on stationery and wedding invitations. Choosing to use the Tara Brooch symbol in wedding decor will honor this ancient Celtic love of ornamentation and craftsmanship.

# A Horseshoe for Good Luck

THE IRISH BELIEVE that horseshoes are a traditional sign of good luck, and many Irish homes around the world display horseshoes over their front doors. In Ireland, blacksmiths often give horseshoes as wedding gifts. Horseshoes are thought to be lucky because "horses were in the stall when Christ was born, and were blessed for evermore," according to Lady Wilde's *Irish Cures, Mystic Charms and Superstitions*. The horseshoe is also thought to bring luck because it is shaped like a crescent moon, which signifies a time of prosperity and good fortune.

It is customary for Irish brides to carry a horseshoe when walking down the aisle. This custom is still practiced today in many parts of Ireland, as it has been for centuries. Many modern-day Irish brides have forgone the custom of carrying a real horseshoe and have opted instead to carry a smaller porcelain or crystal version. Waterford Crystal and Royal Tara Giftware are two Irish companies that carry decorative horseshoes appropriate to carry down the aisle.

Perhaps the easiest way to carry out this tradition is for the bride to get a small silver horseshoe charm and pin it on her wedding dress, next to her heart. Be sure the horseshoe is pinned with the points up, as it is believed that a horseshoe pointed up will catch and hold all good luck.

## The Quilted Ring Bearer's Pillow

IN NINETEENTH-CENTURY Ireland, young women would often prepare for marriage by accumulating household items and linens in a hope chest, also known as the "bottom drawer." Women of a village or urban neighborhood would participate in quilting parties to help a bride-to-be accumulate the quilts and blankets needed to set up her new home. These parties were gay social events that included a meal, some friendly gossip, and often ended with singing and dancing when the men arrived.

This is a tradition that could be modified into a modern-day "quilting" bridal shower. Making an entire quilt may be too time consuming for today's busy women, but a quilted ring bearer's pillow could be put together in an afternoon and would add a lovely homemade touch to the wedding.

Ask guests to bring along a small swatch of fabric to the shower, if possible, one that has some sentimental value. The mother of the groom could bring a bit of her son's christening gown; the bride's best friend could bring a piece of her prom dress. Friends who may not have a piece of fabric with a special history might bring along a bit of Irish lace or an Irish linen handkerchief.

To assemble the pillow, these pieces of fabric can be cut into one-inch squares and arranged in a simple block quilting pattern. For something more elaborate, there are patterns with Celtic designs that can be found at most craft stores that sell quilting materials. If you want the pillow to look more traditional and match the bride's dress, ask guests to bring only white pieces of material or back the quilt with white satin or white Irish linen.

During the party, each guest can sew a few stitches of the quilted square. Having many women work on a bride's bottom drawer was thought to bring her good luck in her marriage. Be sure to play some lively Irish music during the stitching session, which will set the mood. If you are not worried about the quality of the stitching, break out some Irish whiskey—a not unknown occurrence during quilting parties in Belfast. A drop of good whiskey is a sure way to loosen tongues, get the gossip flowing, and ensure a memorable afternoon that the bride-to-be and her friends won't soon forget.

# Irish Flowers

THERE ARE MANY varieties of flowers that grow in Ireland and would be ideal for an Irish wedding. In the Middle Ages, it was believed that herbs would ward off evil spirits, so brides would carry bouquets of herbs and flowers on their wedding day.

Many flowers were assigned meaning in ancient times and were often used symbolically in affairs of the heart, as well as during ancient ceremonies and on the battlefield. In Victorian times, numerous books were printed about the "language of flowers," in which the meanings of individual flowers were presented. These books were popular with cultured ladies of the day.

Here are some of the most popular Irish flowers for weddings, including their meanings, taken from the Victorian era. They can be used in bouquets for the bride and her attendants, as the boutonnieres of the groom and his groomsmen, and also in decorations for the ceremony and reception.

*Burnet Rose*—A white rose that grows wild all over Ireland. Respect is associated with white roses.

*Violets*—The violet denotes faithfulness, and the common wild variety is indigenous to Ireland.

*Hydrangeas*—The gorgeous blue and pink variety of hydrangea can be seen all over the west of Ireland. They symbolize devotion and remembrance, perfect sentiments for a wedding day.

*Pansy*—The delicate seaside pansy is found on Irish soil and "thoughts of you" is its meaning.

*Foxglove*—According to the botany department of the University of Galway, the Irish word for foxglove is *lus na mban side*, which translates as "plant of the fairy women." Include foxgloves to honor Ireland's fairy queens.

*Bells of Ireland*—Add this to a bridal bouquet for a little whimsy, as that is the meaning of this green stalk with delicate white flowers.

*Daisy*—The charming little daisy denotes innocence, and the ox-eye variety of daisy grows wild in many parts of Ireland.

*Elderberry*—The elder is another wildflower of Ireland. Use sprigs of elderberries for some variation in arrangements and bouquets. Elderberries connote warmth and kindness.

*Irish Orchids*—A few Irish orchids woven into the bridal bouquet will add lust and luxury to the marriage.

*Dahlia*—The dahlia is one of the most popular flowers for container growing in Ireland. Dahlias fill the windowboxes of many cottages all across the Irish countryside. Use this flower when making boutonnieres and corsages for parents, as the dahlia denotes gratitude.

*Primrose*—Another flower that is indigenous to Irish soil, the primrose is thought to ward off evil. Lady Wilde reveals that "evil spirits cannot touch anything guarded by primroses, if they are plucked before sunrise."

*Ferns*—Ferns signify sincerity and were an important ingredient in medieval love potions. Killarney ferns are grown in Ireland, and sprays of this plant would add a nice green accompaniment to bouquets and arrangements.

*Ivy*—In Ireland ivy is very popular for use in bridal bouquets and the centerpieces for the reception. Trailing ivy will give the tables a feel of outdoor gardens and secret fairy forests. Ivy is perhaps the most appropriate plant or flower to use for marriage, as its meaning is wedded love.

# A Sprig of Mint

THE FOLLOWING SUPERSTITION appeared in Lady Wilde's book *Irish Cures, Mystic Charms and Superstitions*. It was believed that if one wanted to inspire love, a sprig of mint should be held until it grew moist. A lover was to then clasp the hand of his or her intended. The love would be returned as long as the two hands were closed over the herb.

This old legend can be re-created on a couple's wedding day. The bride might tuck a sprig of mint into her bridal bouquet and, during the ceremony when the couple is reciting their vows, slip the sprig of mint into her groom's hand. This will undoubtedly ensure a lifetime of love.

# A Bible Bouquet

BRIDES IN NORTHERN Ireland will often carry a Bible when they walk down the aisle, instead of the traditional bridal bouquet. The Bible is often bound in white leather to match the bride's wedding dress. Many families will have a Bible that has been passed down for generations, and carrying an heirloom is a way for a bride to honor her family. To carry out this custom but still add a decorative touch, the

Bible can be embellished with ribbons and fresh flowers. To do this, cut ribbons in a variety of lengths from two feet to five feet. Tie a flower on both ends of each ribbon. Flowers with sturdy stems, such as roses, will work best and last longer. It is also possible to use dried or fabric flowers.

If using fresh flowers, keep them refrigerated until leaving for the ceremony. When ready to leave, place the ribbons between the pages of the Bible, using them as a bookmark. The trailing ribbons will give the Bible the look of a cascading bouquet.

If the bride has a favorite Bible passage, it would be a lovely gesture to mark it for her using the ribbons. The bride may want to read the passage for inspiration as she travels to the ceremony or right before she walks down the aisle.

## Harvest Love Knots

THE CUSTOM OF making harvest knots comes from the farming community in Northern Ireland. Young men and women would take long plaits of straw and twist them into decorative knots. These harvest knots were then given as love tokens to be worn on a lapel. Women would also wear the knots woven in their hair. When one gave a harvest knot to a lover, it was considered a sign of a committed relation-ship and it was assumed that a wedding would follow in the spring.

Harvest love knots can be included in an Irish wedding in many different ways. A knot can be embellished with flowers and worn as a boutonniere by the groom. They can also be incorporated into a crown of fresh flowers to be worn in the bride's hair. Love knots can be attached to the bride's bouquet with colorful ribbons as an added decorative touch or be used as napkin rings at place settings during the reception meal.

## MAKING A HARVEST LOVE KNOT

Harvest knots were originally made from straw that was freshly cut and very pliable. If you have access to fresh hay or wheat, you can try to make the love knot in one of these materials. A simple way to make the knot is to use a natural raffia, available in craft stores. For a smaller, more delicate harvest knot, try using a 30-gauge floral wire in natural.

1. Cut nine pieces of raffia fifteen inches long.

2. Separate into three groups of three and braid each group separately.

3. Take the three braided raffia and braid together into one strand.

4. Twist the large braided strand into a double loop and then use an additional piece of raffia to tie the ends together directly beneath the double loop.

5. You can now tie a sprig of wheat to the harvest knot with a colored ribbon, or attach a fresh flower with additional raffia if you are making a boutonniere.

The Irish peasants were very creative when making gifts for a loved one. Feel free to try different variations of the harvest knot by adding thicker strands of raffia or using different types of straw and wheat.

## Decorating the Path

WHEN IT CAME to celebrating a wedding in nineteenth-century Ireland, the entire village would often get involved, especially if the couple to be married was of a high social standing. The morning of a wedding, the streets from the bride's house to the church would be decorated with floral garlands or evergreen boughs that would arch across the couple's path. Sometimes the decoration would also include lit lanterns or burning torches.

This is a useful custom to practice for today's weddings, as it helps guests find their way to the church or from the church to the wedding reception. The decoration can be as elaborate as fancy floral arrangements attached to trees and signposts or as simple as colored balloons or bows to lead the way. Reproductions of a map of Ireland, a picture of an Irish cottage, or the symbol of a shamrock or harp in bright colors might also be attached to the trees and signposts.

Be sure to get permission to put decorations on private property. Most land and home owners will be happy to accommodate the request when they hear the decoration is for a wedding party, and getting neighbors involved is in keeping with this old Irish custom.

## Irish Wedding Attire

"THREE EXCELLENCES OF Dress," states the old Irish triad, "elegance, comfort, and lastingness." These are three qualities that the Irish have aspired to in their clothing, especially for an occasion like a wedding.

In the nineteenth century, society was divided between the aristocratic and farming classes. Only very wealthy brides of a high social class could afford to wear the traditional white bridal gown, which was made popular by Queen Victoria. The average bride of the farming class would choose an outfit that could be worn again, often a two-piece skirt and top or a nice dress in a sensible fabric. Men of both classes wore their best suits.

At the beginning of the twentieth century, inspired by the coronation of Edward VII, wedding fashions became more relaxed and even a bit frivolous. Many brides chose to wear hats instead of veils. Lace and chiffon replaced gowns of stiff satin. This trend continued until the Second World War, when most Irish women chose to wear a simple suit, there being little money for lavish weddings during wartime.

Today brides in Ireland are usually married in a traditional white wedding gown, and grooms in tuxedos or suits. Irish bridal designers are known for their simple yet elegant made-to-order designs.

Here are some ideas for adding Irish-inspired touches to wedding attire.

## EMBROIDERY

Many of the top bridal designers in Ireland embellish wedding dresses with embroidery in an Irish or Celtic theme. Celtic designs—shamrocks, a coat of arms, even a harp or Irish flower—can be embroidered on the bodice or along the sleeves and hem of a wedding dress. Grooms can have ties or vests embroidered with these same designs. These embroidered emblems can be repeated in the attire of the wedding party.

Embroidery on wedding attire goes back more than a century. Queen Victoria had her wedding dress embroidered with symbols for each of her kingdoms. These included the Tudor rose of England, the leek of Wales, the shamrock of Ireland, and the thistle of Scotland.

To find a source for embroidery, check with companies that specialize in monogramming. Tailors who make Irish dance costumes are another good source, as embroidery is often used on dance competition outfits. These tailors will be very familiar with Irish and Celtic embroidery designs.

## WEDDING VEILS

Like brides in most parts of the world, Irish brides wear a bridal veil as part of their wedding attire. Long ago, a bride would be veiled to hide her away from evil spirits, which in Ireland included the pesky leprechauns and fairies who would try to capture a bride for her fine dress. A veil was also thought to represent purity and chastity in ancient times.

According to Lady Wilde, couples in rural Ireland would be veiled in heavy black cloth at the beginning of their wedding ceremony. This represented the mystery of love, shrouded and veiled from the prying light of day. At the end of the marriage rite, the couple would then circle the altar three times. The veil would be lifted as the couple sealed their wedding vows with a kiss.

Many brides in Ireland wear bridal veils that have been embellished with embroidery. Shamrocks or the Claddagh symbol are two popular emblems often embroidered on Irish wedding veils.

## TIARAS

In recent years brides in Ireland have enhanced their wedding veils with a decorative tiara. Tiaras are a tribute to an Irish bride's Celtic ancestors and add a special beauty to wedding attire.

Celtic men and women of higher classes wore a crown, commonly known as a "minn," for special occasions. Minns were quite elaborately made and could be expensive, depending on the rank the wearer had in a Celtic clan. Irish kings had crowns of gold, jewels, and enamel. A thirteenth-century fresco painting of the O'Connors, kings of Connaght, shows fine examples of the decorated Irish crowns on the heads of the clan's leaders.

Today, Irish tiara designers are using gold, silver, crystals, and pearls on their tiaras. Some are even using the *Book of Kells* for inspiration in their designs.

## THE KINSALE CLOAK

If marrying during the winter months, a bride may want to consider a cape to cover her wedding gown. The Kinsale, or Kerry, cloak, a full-length cape with a hood, was worn by country women in the west of Ireland during the 1800s. The traditional cape was made of water-resistant lamb's wool from the local sheep of Cork and Kerry. Today, capes are made in silks and velvets, in an array of colors, including red, which was a popular color for cloaks in Galway.

## SHOES

It may be surprising to learn that the Irish believe it's lucky to get married in a pair of old shoes. There are different explanations for this custom. In Cork it is believed that fairies would whisk away a bride and groom to Tir Na N'Og, the Land of the Ever Young, just to get a hold of a pair of handsome new slippers.

The custom may also come from the idea of beginning a new journey with something familiar, like a favorite pair of broken-in shoes. The old shoe custom can be useful—buying a pair of shoes months before your wedding and breaking them in properly will ensure a wedding day devoid of sore feet.

Another way the Irish incorporate old shoes is to tie them to the bumper of the newlywed's car, much as Americans use tin cans. This notion came about because leather was thought to protect against evil spirits, and shoes are also thought to ensure fertility. *Wedding Guide UK* offers up the answer that shoes mean fertility by giving an example of Mother Goose's extremely prolific little old woman who lived in a shoe!

## THE LAST STITCH

One last Irish custom with regard to attire comes from the countryside in Cork. It is believed that the last stitch of a bride's wedding dress should be sewn on the morning of the wedding to ensure a lucky marriage.

# Irish Lace

A BRIDE MAY want to embellish her wedding attire with lace handmade in Ireland. Two kinds of lace making, needle-point and bobbin, were introduced to Ireland in the late seventeenth century. It is believed that these lace-making techniques were learned first by nuns whose convents were affiliated with monasteries in France.

Lace making expanded during the Great Famine, when many Irish convents taught the skill to local women as a means of income to relieve starvation. For the women of Ireland, lace making was a symbol of life, hope, and pride.

The height of the lace-making period was 1900 to 1914.

The peak came in 1907, according to Ada Longfeld's book *Irish Lace*. Lady Aberdeen, a patron of many lace-making associations, threw the Vice-Regal Lace Ball, in which even the men attending were required to wear some handmade Irish lace. Lace making grew less common as the twentieth century continued, when many of the great craftswomen grew older and eventually died.

Happily, however, today there has been a revival in lace making. County Monaghan is known as the lace-making county of Ireland, with the Clones Lace Guild at its center. The guild takes commissions for pieces of lace and lace veils. There is also the Lace Museum in the small village of Ballanaleck, which has a shop that sells antique lace.

Carrickmacross lace is also quite popular today. The lace designs are embroidered on a very fine net backing, which makes it easy to attach the lacework to a wedding dress's bodice or sleeve. If you commission lace, allow about three months for a veil and less time for a smaller piece. The price will depend on the size of the piece and the amount of detail in the design. According to the Carrick-macross Lace Gallery in County Monaghan, British royalty from Queen Victoria to Princess Diana have commissioned pieces of this finely crafted lace for their wedding dresses.

Kenmare lace is the very fine needlepoint style of lace that was passed down to the local women from the nuns at Clare Convent in Kenmare, County Kerry. Today, the

Kenmare Lace and Design Center continues the Kenmare lace tradition with five ladies who will take commissions for small pieces of lace. They have created a lace brooch that would look lovely on a wedding dress with a high Victorian neck. The center also sells lace–making kits, giving enthusiasts an opportunity to create their own piece of Kenmare lace.

## Payment of Tinnscra

THE ANCIENT BREHON laws in Ireland stated that before a man and woman could wed, the groom must offer up "tinnscra" or a bride–price to the father of the bride. It was believed that each person had a value, and when a bride was taken from her family, her value must be compensated. The bride–price could be paid with cattle, land, horses, or gold and silver.

This custom was carried out well into the twentieth century. When marriages were arranged by matchmakers, there was often some form of compensation made to the bride or her family.

This would be a joyous custom to re–create during the rehearsal dinner; often a time for the families to come together in an intimate setting and honor the bride and groom. The groom can make a toast to his new family,

explaining the ancient tinnscra custom. He can then ceremoniously offer an Irish coin as payment for his new bride,
ensuring their future happiness.

## Grooms Gifts

IT IS CUSTOMARY in Ireland for the groom to give the
bride and her bridesmaids a gift of jewelry on the morning
of the wedding. Society pages in Irish newspapers from the
turn of the century include detailed mention of grooms gifts,
often gold bracelets and necklaces. This custom is still
widely practiced in Ireland today, and often grooms will give
jewelry with a Celtic theme.

As a special remembrance of the day and in keeping with
the Irish theme of the wedding, the groom can find earrings
with harps or shamrocks, or possibly a Claddagh pendant or
bracelet. There is also a wide selection of jewelry, with
designs taken from the *Book of Kells,* manufactured by
numerous Irish and American companies.

Since it is customary in the United States to give wedding gifts to the entire wedding party, the bride can also give
gifts to the groomsmen. If the bride would like to continue
the tradition of giving jewelry, cufflinks and tie pins are
available with Irish themes. Groomsmen can also be given a
key chain with an Irish design or a silver flask engraved

with their initials in Celtic-style lettering—and filled with Irish whiskey.

## Fiddlers and Pipers

IN CENTURIES PAST, the bridal party would often walk in a procession to and from the church led by a fiddle player, who would play a variety of joyous tunes, always including "Haste to the Wedding" in his repertoire.

If your reception is close to the church, having a fiddler lead the wedding party and guests out of the church and to the reception hall will add much revelry to the day and create a festive atmosphere.

Bagpipers are also used to escort brides into the church. Even though bagpipes originated in Scotland, this custom is very popular at modern-day Irish weddings. Some couples will opt for a piper who plays uilleann pipes, an Irish bagpipe, as those are considered more authentically Irish. The piper often plays right outside the reception hall to welcome guests. Pipers will also officially present a couple to the guests at the reception by leading them into the reception dinner.

# Jaunting Carts

ON THE ISLE of Inishmore in the west of Ireland, bridal parties will ride to the church in horse-drawn jaunting carts. The carts and horses are sometimes decorated with colorful ribbons and flowers. It becomes quite a spectacle on the island when a wedding party passes. This tradition was born out of necessity, as there are very few cars on Inishmore.

This mode of transportation for the bride and groom was popular all over Ireland in the nineteenth century. Even the horses were spruced up for a wedding day. Horses' manes, and even their ears, would be decorated with ribbons and dangling tassels.

To hire jaunting carts or carriages drawn by horses for your wedding, check with stables that board horses in your area. Stables or possibly local farmers are most likely to have carts that look most like the traditional Irish jaunting cart. You can also check your local bridal magazines for horse-drawn carriages, though these are often very elaborate Cinderella-style affairs and also tend to be expensive.

When decorating the horses and carts, use the same flowers used in your bridal bouquet, which will be another nice touch if the flowers are indigenous to Ireland. Ribbons in the bridal colors can also be braided into the horses' manes for a colorful flourish.

# VOWS AND BLESSINGS

Planning an Irish
Wedding Ceremony

OF ALL THE THINGS YOU must do to prepare for
your wedding, planning the ceremony can be the most
daunting. Declaring your love and commitment in front of
friends and family is a very public declaration of often very
private feelings, but with the proper preparation, creating
the ceremony will become one of the fondest memories of
your entire wedding experience.

Ireland's poetic tradition is perhaps the greatest gift from
our ancestors, and the wedding ceremony is the perfect
place to instill a bit of the Irish. This chapter will present
Celtic ceremonies derived from Ireland's ancient past, peas-

ant traditions from the last century, and traditions and customs that are practiced in Ireland today. You will also find a selection of Irish blessings, prayers, and offerings that can be incorporated into the ceremony, as well as some ideas for Irish music that would be appropriate for the wedding ceremony.

As a theme, love is one that the Irish do spectacularly well, and as you will see in this chapter, the Irish have given us some of the most beautiful words from the heart. Planning your ceremony will be a quiet reflective moment during the often hectic preparations for your wedding. May you delight in the following Irish customs and writings, and in finding the perfect declaration of love.

# The Caim

A CAIM IS an early Celtic Christian custom that can be used to begin an Irish wedding ceremony. Celtic Christians would draw a circle around themselves as a sign of unity with God. The circle was a symbol of the encircling of God's love and the "Mighty Three." The following incantation has multiple meanings. It refers to the Father, Son, and Holy Spirit, as well as the trinity of sky, earth, and water, which are three sacred elements in Celtic tradition. This prayer, from David Adam's book *The Eye of the Eagle*, can be repeated as the circle is drawn.

## A CAIM PRAYER

*The Mighty Three,*
*My protection be.*
*Encircling me.*
*You are around,*
*My life,*
*My love,*
*My home,*
*Encircling me.*
*O sacred Three,*
*The Mighty Three.*

This circle can be drawn in the ground with a birch branch if the wedding is outdoors. If the wedding is inside, or you do not want to disturb the natural habitation, create a garland using flowers and ivy. This garland can be placed in a circle around the couple as the prayer is recited.

At the end of the wedding rite, before the couple breaks the circle, a final Caim prayer can be offered.

## THE PRAYER OF UNION

*We ask the maker*
*Of the sky,*
*Of the earth,*
*Of the water,*
*To encircle this couple.*

*May God surround them with his love*
*And protect them today and every day,*
*As they stand together in holy unity.*

## TO ENSURE A WEALTH OF LOVE

This custom was practiced on the Aran Islands at the turn of the twentieth century. On entering their church, the bride and groom would kneel at the altar rail and place their wedding bands on two half—crowns of silver. This was done to ensure a wealth of love in the marriage. It was also to show appreciation to the officiant performing the ceremony, as the coins were often left for payment.

This custom can be updated using two silver Irish pounds, which can be acquired from any foreign currency exchange. With the blessing of the rings, the officiant invokes the wealth of love these rings symbolize.

*Take these rings off silver crown,*
*A symbol that your heart is bound.*
*To ensure a wealth of Love,*
*Take these rings from Heaven above.*

Once blessed by your officiant, these coins will become your first family heirloom, in honor of your union as husband and wife. Save these coins in a special place and one day you may present them to your children to be used in their weddings. It's wonderful to think of the wealth of love these coins will acquire as they are passed down from generation to generation of happy marriages.

You may also want to display these coins in a shadow box as a daily reminder of the many riches of love that you acquired on your wedding day.

# The Irish Hanky

THE IRISH, BEING an emotional people, have a tradition or two when it comes to shedding a tear. Irish brides carry a linen handkerchief down the aisle to catch their bridal tears. This custom was most likely started by the linen industry in Northern Ireland. Many linen companies suggest that these linen handkerchiefs be used after the wedding to create a christening bonnet for a couple's first baby.

A handkerchief passed down from relatives would also be a lovely touch, as it has a family history and carries generations of a family's tears. Tying a piece of rosemary to the corner of the family hanky will symbolize remembrance of those who used it in the past.

Handkerchiefs can also be presented to the mothers of the bride and groom at the beginning of the service. There are Irish companies that make embroidered linen hankies embellished with shamrocks that come with a special poem honoring mothers, thanking them for making the day special.

A mother will cherish this special gift and will most likely put it to immediate use!

# In Honor of Those Passed

THE SPIRIT OF those departed is most important to the Irish. There are two feast days in Ireland devoted to the dead, Garland Sunday, the first Sunday in September, and All Souls' Day, November 2.

Garland Sunday is an ancient Celtic tradition; a solemn ceremony that the Celts would perform to honor their dead kindred. According to legend, a hoop or wreath made of twigs was decorated with flowers and ribbons by unmarried girls, for the touch of a married woman's hand would bring bad luck. Prayers were then said over the garlands at the grave sites.

All Souls' was a feast day celebrated by the ancient church of Ireland. It was a popular belief that the departed returned to visit their homes once a year on this day. A candle was put in the window for each person who had passed, to show them the way back home.

Both the garland and the lighting of a candle can be incorporated into the wedding ceremony to honor those recently passed. This is especially nice if a mother or father of the bride or groom is gone; it is a lovely way to honor them. A garland is presented to the bride and groom by another family member and then put around an unlit candle. The candle is then lit by the family member, with a few memories spoken about those who have recently departed, including how happy they would be on the bride and groom's wedding day.

# Irish Music for the Ceremony

MUSIC HISTORIAN CIARAN Carson has called Irish music "an expression of the national spirit." There is no better way for a couple to celebrate their heritage on their wedding day than by including some traditional Irish music in the ceremony.

What first comes to mind when one thinks of Irish music are the faced-paced reels, jigs, and waltzes of an Irish dance band. This music will add merriment to the reception, but there are also many ballads and traditional airs that are beautiful and more appropriate for the wedding ceremony.

The harp is the national symbol of Ireland, and including a harpist is one way to honor tradition. Most harp players have a repertoire of Irish tunes, and harp music can be used to set the mood as guests arrive for the ceremony. It is also lovely during transitional points—during processionals, recessionals, or during communion, if it is a part of the ceremony.

Another tradition in Irish music is the soloist or group singing a cappella. The pure sound of voices with no musical accompaniment can be quite haunting and lovely during a wedding ceremony. A song sung in Irish would also follow tradition.

To find singers, check Irish newspapers, if you have them in your area, or contact the music department of local colleges. They will be able to direct you to local Irish singers and musicians. You can also try local churches, which often have choral groups that will hire out for weddings.

Here are some suggestions of Irish music that could be included in the wedding ceremony.

### Turlough O'Carolan

O'Carolan was a beloved Irish composer and harpist from the eighteenth century. Blinded by smallpox at the age of eighteen, O'Carolan traveled Ireland composing tunes for the Irish gentry. Over two hundred of his melodies have survived, which he originally composed for the harp. He would often compose tunes in honor of weddings; so it would be very fitting to include an O'Carolan piece in your wedding ceremony.

### "In This Heart"

WRITTEN AND PERFORMED BY SINEAD O'CONNOR. Although a modern piece written in English, it is performed in the traditional *Sean-nos* or "old style." A song about finding true love that sounds best when sung a cappella by a quartet of voices and that is perfect for a wedding.

### "The Rose of Tralee"

WRITTEN BY CHARLES GLOVER, MORDAUNT SPENSER. This classic Irish ballad is one of Ireland's best-loved songs.

### "Ned of the Hill"

WRITTEN BY L. LOVER. A traditional piece that works well as a solo for one voice or accompanied by a harp, fiddle, or tin whistle.

### "She Moved Through the Fair"

LYRICS BY PADRAIC COLUM, MUSIC BY HERBERT HUGHES. The lyrics of this traditional tune suggest a man who has lost his lover, but the song has become so popular for Irish weddings that the lyrics have taken on a new positive meaning for those about to marry.

### "My Lagan Love"

TRADITIONAL, AUTHOR UNKNOWN. This haunting ballad conjures a mythical love from the sea.

### "My Wild Irish Rose"

WRITTEN BY CHAUNCEY OLCOTT. Olcott wrote many songs with Irish themes in the 1920s. This was a popular ballad sung on many vaudeville stages.

### "When Irish Eyes Are Smiling"

WRITTEN BY CHAUNCEY OLCOTT. The most famous of Olcott's Irish tunes. Originally written for vaudeville, it became an anthem for Irish everywhere when Bing Crosby recorded it.

### "I Know Where I'm Going"

WRITTEN BY BOOSEY AND HAWKES. An Ulster folk tune about a young girl thinking of love and whom she will marry.

### "The Irish Wedding Song"

WRITTEN BY IAN BETTERIDGE. Betteridge is an Australian singer/songwriter. This is not a traditional Irish tune but must be mentioned because of its huge popularity in Ireland, as well as America, Canada, and Australia.

Here is a list of up-tempo, joyous Irish tunes that would be appropriate for the recessional. They are a lively way to end the ceremony, getting everyone in the mood for a party.

### "Marie's Wedding"

TRADITIONAL, AUTHOR UNKNOWN

*"Haste to the Wedding"*
WRITTEN BY O'NEIL, FIRST NAME UNKNOWN

*"Star of the County Down"*
WRITTEN BY TOM KINES, AND VIA KEL.

*"I'll Tell Me Ma" ("The Bell of Belfast City")*
TRADITIONAL, AUTHOR UNKNOWN

*"Sweet Rosie O'Grady"*
WRITTEN BY MAUDE NUGENT

Sheet music for these classic Irish songs can usually be found in larger libraries with a music department, or check with musical instrument retailers, who often sell sheet music.

# The Oathing Stone

IN IRELAND THERE are many sacred stones around which spiritual devotions and ancient rituals took place. Tara was the meeting place of the ancient kings of Ireland. At this ancient site, there still stands a sacred stone that is said to mark the place where the ancient kings were sworn in as leaders.

Stones, being part of the earth, were thought to hold the memories of Irish ancestors. To make a binding oath on or near an ancient stone was to make a powerful and lasting vow, as if your vows were "carved in stone."

This Celtic tradition can be re-created at a couple's wedding ceremony. A small stone can be acquired from Ireland, perhaps a piece of Connemara marble, which is available in many Irish gift shops, but any stone from Irish soil will do. While reciting their wedding vows, the couple can place their hands on this stone. The oathing stone will be a strong symbol of a couple's hardfast commitment to each other and their future lives together.

## Ancient Celtic Vows

CELTIC CHRISTIANITY, AS well as an interest in the history of the Celts, has become popular with many people of Irish descent. It is now possible to find ancient Celtic vows and rituals to incorporate into your wedding. Morgan Llywelyn is a historical novelist who specializes in Celtic culture. In her book *Finn MacCool*, she has translated the following wedding vows from the ancient brehon law. To Llywelyn, these vows are an example of what a loving marriage should represent.

These vows can be recited by the bride and groom one at a time or repeated together at the prompting of the officiant, who was known in ancient Ireland as a Druid, one of a special group of men and women who were the most holy and learned of their tribe.

## BRIDE AND GROOM

*You cannot possess me for I belong to myself.*
*But while we both wish it, I give you that which is mine to*
    *give.*
*You cannot command me for I am a free person.*
*But I shall serve you in those ways you require*
*And the honeycomb will taste sweeter coming from my*
    *hand.*
*I pledge to you that yours will be the name I cry aloud in the*
    *night.*
*And the eyes into which I smile in the morning.*
*I pledge to you the first bite from my meat*
*And the first drink from my cup.*
*I pledge to you my living and my dying, equally in your care.*
*And tell no strangers our grievances.*
*This is my wedding vow to you.*
*This is a marriage of equals.*

After these vows are spoken, the officiating Druid recites the following.

*These promises you make by the sun and moon,*
*By fire and water, by day and night, by land and sea.*
*With these vows you swear, by the Gods your people swear*
*   by,*
*To be full partners, each to the other.*
*If one drops the load, the other will pick it up.*
*If one is discredited to the other, his own honor will be*
*   forfeit,*
*Generation upon generation,*
*Until he repairs that which was damaged*
*And finds that which was lost.*
*The vow of first degree supersedes all others.*
*Shall you fail to keep the oath you pledge today,*
*The elements themselves will reach out and destroy you.*

That marriage is a covenant between equals is perhaps the most beautiful idea to be taken from these ancient vows by Llywelyn. They can be incorporated into a more traditional wedding service, in part or in whole.

# A Handfasting Ceremony

HANDFASTING IS A type of Celtic wedding ceremony from the Middle Ages. It was a temporary marriage that lasted for a year and was a trial period for couples to cohabit. Handfasting was considered a simple secular ritual that could be performed by the couple without an officiant present. Their pledge to each other was the binding power; a couple needed no other authority but their mutual commitment.

At the end of one year, couples who chose to stay together had a second, permanent handfasting ceremony. Today, handfasting can be legally binding if performed by an officiant with state qualifications to marry.

For this handfasting ceremony, written by Celtic spiritualist Lady Ardane, the guests stand in a circle with the bride and groom in the middle. The ceremony is known as a handfasting because of the cord used during the ceremony to bind the couple together. The expression "tying the knot" is believed to come from handfasting rituals.

### HIGH PRIEST

We gather here this day to bind together this man and woman in a ritual of love. Let all who stand within this circle be filled with love. May this sacred space be consecrated before the gods and goddesses. Let _____ and _____ stand before us in the presence of the ancient ones.

The High Priest walks to the east side of the circle.

### HIGH PRIEST

Be with us here, Spirits of the Air, with your breath of life join the bonds between these two and tie them tightly.

The High Priest walks to the south side of the circle.

**HIGH PRIEST**

Be with us here, Beings of Fire. Give their love and passion your own all-consuming ardor.

The High Priest walks to the west side of the circle.

**HIGH PRIEST**

Be with us here, Beings of Water. Grant these two the deepest love, richness of body, soul, and spirit.

The High Priest walks to the north side of the circle.

**HIGH PRIEST**

Be with us here, Spirits of Earth. Let your strength and constancy be theirs for as long as they desire to be together.

The High Priest returns to the couple.

**HIGH PRIEST**

Blessed Goddess and Laughing God, look with joy on the union of this man and this woman. Grant them harmony and beauty in their lives and let them always be mindful of their commitment, one to the other. Let their joy of each other be a shining beacon for all to see.

The High Priest loops the couple's wedding rings through a golden handfasting cord and holds it above his or her head for all to see.

**HIGH PRIEST**

Above you the stars, below you the stones. As time passes, remember this: Like a stone your love should be firm; be close, yet not so close that you restrict one another. Have patience with each other for storms may come, but they will quickly go.

The High Priest gives the bride's ring to the groom.

HIGH PRIEST

Is it your wish to become one with this woman?

GROOM

That is my wish.

HIGH PRIEST

Place the ring on your beloved's finger and repeat the following: "Let this circle of gold reflect the circle in which we stand, to be the constant reminder of the pledges exchanged. Let it remind us daily of the wheel of life and the unbroken cycles of eternity."

The High Priest repeats this with the bride. The High Priest then asks the bride and groom to face each other and hold hands. He binds the couple's hands with the golden cord.

HIGH PRIEST

As we bind together this man and woman with this golden cord, let their fates and future be so bound. May they hold fast to each other, ever as they are now held fast. As the God and Goddess and the ancient ones are witness to these rites, I now proclaim you to be wed to each other.

The bride and groom kiss.

We dismiss you now, O spirits of air, earth, fire, and water. We ask you to return to your elemental home, harming none as you go and taking with you our thanks for your attendance.

# The Celtic Loving Cup

THE IRISH ARE famous for their toasts. Ask anyone with an ounce of Irish in them, and they can probably come up with a bit of goodwill and good luck in the form of an Irish toast. The idea of raising a glass to offer best wishes has a long history in Celtic tradition.

By the fifteenth century it was common for the Celtic peoples to toast each other with a ceremonial cup. In Scotland this cup is know as a *quaich*, which comes from the Gaelic word *cuach*, meaning cup. A very romantic version of the loving cup was a *quaich* that had a double glass bottom, in which was kept a lock of a loved one's hair. The celebrant would be offering a toast to his loved one every time his glass was raised.

Today there are different versions of the Celtic loving cup. The traditional *quaich* is shaped like a two-handled bowl and often has an inlaid Celtic

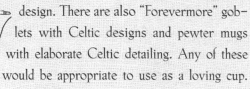

design. There are also "Forevermore" goblets with Celtic designs and pewter mugs with elaborate Celtic detailing. Any of these would be appropriate to use as a loving cup. Perhaps your family has an heirloom piece of Irish crystal that could be borrowed for the ceremony.

The purpose of the loving cup ceremony is for the bride and groom to share their first drink together as man and wife. The cup is then passed down from generation to generation, ensuring happiness and good fortune to all who drink from it. This is a special moment for the couple to toast their love, devotion, and friendship.

The Celtic understanding of friendship finds its inspiration in the notion of an *anam cara*. John O'Donohue, in his book of the same title, explains that the Gaelic *anam* is translated as soul, and *cara* is the Gaelic word for friend. An *anam cara* is therefore your "soul friend," the person with whom you share the most hidden intimacies of your life.

What follows are some of the beautiful thoughts found in O'Donohue's *Anam Cara*, which have been used to create the following Loving Cup Ceremony. This ceremony could be included as part of your wedding vows, or possibly performed informally at the reception, when your guests are offering up toasts. Please note, I based this ceremony on O'Donohue's work; it does not originate with him.

# Celtic Loving Cup Ceremony

**OFFICIANT/FRIEND**

On this your wedding day, we celebrate the Celtic spirit of the *anam cara*. *Anam cara* is translated from the Gaelic as "soul friend." By entering in a partnership with your *anam cara*, you are joined in an ancient and eternal way with this person whom you most cherish. In everyone's life there is a great need for an *anam cara* and so I ask you to toast one another by repeating the following.

The bride and groom hold the loving cup as they repeat the following.

**BRIDE/GROOM**

Today I recognize you, my *anam cara*

And ask that you become a part of me, in sacred kinship.

With you I will share my innermost self, my mind and my heart.

With you, I have lost all fear and have found the greatest courage.

I have learned to love and let myself be loved.

With you, I have found a rhythm of grace and gracefulness.

Love has reawakened in my life; a rebirth; a new beginning.

With you my *anam cara,*

I am understood,

I am home.

OFFICIANT/FRIEND

And now, please drink to the love you've shared in the past.

The couple takes turns sipping from the loving cup.

OFFICIANT/FRIEND

Drink to your love in the present, on this your wedding day.

The couple drinks.

OFFICIANT/FRIEND

And drink to your love in the future and forever more.

The couple drinks.

OFFICIANT/FRIEND

The Celts believed that the way you view your future actually shapes it. I now ask everyone here in the room to take a
moment to visualize a future for the bride and groom. As a
group let's think of the happiness in store for _____ and
_____ . Let's put their joyous future out to the universe.

A moment of silence is taken. The officiant then offers
his own blessing, or if the loving cup ceremony is held during the reception, the officiant can offer a final toast.

*"Slainte!"*

*Slainte* is Irish for "to your health" and is the equivalent of saying "cheers" in this country.

# Irish Poetry

THE WEDDING CEREMONY is a wonderful time to include some Irish poetry. The bride and groom may each choose a special love poem that conveys their feelings for the other. There are many superb collections of Irish love poetry currently in print. When looking for the right piece, remember that a poem need not be a literal interpretation of a person's life but should convey the beauty and essence of a couple's feelings of love.

Once a poem is chosen, strong consideration should be given to who will read it. A friend or family member who is comfortable speaking in public is the best option. Perhaps there is an Irish friend or relative who can give the poem some authentic Irish spirit.

The couple should explain to the reader why this particular poem was chosen. The reader is much more likely to convey a couple's feelings of joy if he or she understands the bride or groom's passion for the poem.

Here are a few love poems by some of Ireland's greatest poets. May you be inspired by the following to search for the perfect Irish declaration of love.

# 'TIS ALL FOR THEE

*If life for me hath joy or light,*
*'Tis all for thee,*
*My thoughts by day, my dreams by night,*
*Are but of thee, of only thee.*
*Whate'er of hope or peace I know,*
*My zest in joy, my balm in woe,*
*To those dear eyes of thine I owe,*
*'Tis all from thee.*

*My heart, ev'n ere I saw those eyes,*
*Seem'd doom'd to thee;*
*Kept pure till then from other ties,*
*'Twas all for thee, for only thee.*
*Like plants that sleep, till sunny May*
*Calls forth their life, my spirit lay,*
*Till touch'd by Love's awak'ning ray,*
*It liv'd for thee, it liv'd for thee.*

*When Fame would call me to her heights,*
*She speaks by thee;*
*And dim would shine her proudest lights,*
*Unshar'd by thee, unshar'd by thee.*
*Whene'er I seek the Muse's shrine,*
*Where Bards have hung their wreaths divine,*
*And wish those wreaths of glory mine,*
*'Tis all for thee, for only thee.*

—THOMAS MOORE (1779–1852)

## EXCERPT FROM *THE WINGS OF LOVE*

*I will row my boat on Muckross Lake when the gray of the*
    *dove*
*Comes down at the end of the day; and quiet like a prayer*
*Grows soft in your eyes, and among your fluttering hair*
*The red of the sun is mixed with the red of your cheek*
*I will row you, O boat of my heart! till our mouths have*
    *forgotten to speak.*
*In the silence of love, broken only by trout that spring*
*And are gone, like a fairy's finger that casts a ring*
*With the luck of the world for the hand that can hold it fast.*
*I will rest my oars, my eyes on your eyes, till our thoughts*
    *have passed*
*From the lake and the sky and the rings of the jumping fish;*
*Till our ears are filled from the reeds with a sudden swish,*
*And sound like the beating of flails in the time of corn.*
*We shall hold our breath while a wonderful thing is born*
*From the songs that were chanted by bards in the days gone*
    *by . . .*

—JAMES H. COUSINS (b. 1873)

*I give thee all—I can no more—*
*Though poor the off'ring be;*
*My heart and lute are all the store*
*That I can bring to thee.*
*A lute whose gentle song reveals*
*The soul of love full well;*
*And, better far, a heart that feels*
*Much more than lute could tell.*

*Though love and song may fail alas!*
*To keep life's clouds away,*
*At least 'twill make them lighter pass*
*Or gild them if they stay.*
*And ev'n if care, at moments, flings*
*A discord o'er life's happy strain,*
*Let love but gently touch the strings,*
*'Twill all be sweet again!*

—THOMAS MOORE (1779–1852)

## A DRINKING SONG

*Wine comes in the mouth*
*And love comes in the eye;*
*That's all we should know for truth*
*Before we grow old and die.*
*I lift the glass to my mouth,*
*I look at you, and sigh.*

—WILLIAM BUTLER YEATS (1865–1939)

## THE HEART OF A WOMAN

*O what to me the little room*
*That was brimmed up with prayer and rest;*
*He bade me out into the gloom,*
*And my breast lies upon his breast.*

*O what to me my mother's care,*
*The house where I was safe and warm;*
*The shadowy blossom of my hair*
*Will hide us from the bitter storm.*

*O hiding hair and dewy eyes,*
*I am no more with life and death,*
*My heart upon his warm heart lies,*
*My breath is mixed into his breath.*

—WILLIAM BUTLER YEATS (1865–1939)

## "OH, CALL IT BY SOME BETTER NAME"

*Oh call it by some better name,*
*For friendship sounds too cold,*
*While Love is now a worldly flame,*
*Whose shrine must be of gold;*
*And Passion, like the sun at noon,*
*That burns o'er all he sees,*
*Awhile as warm, will set as soon*
*Then, call it none of these.*

*Imagine something purer far,*
*More free from stain of clay*
*Than Friendship, Love, or Passion are,*
*Yet human still as they:*
*And if thy lip, for love like this,*
*No mortal word can frame,*
*Go, ask of angels what it is,*
*And call it by that name!*

—THOMAS MOORE (1779–1852)

# The Bell of Truce

RINGING THE BELL of truce is a custom that can be performed as part of the wedding ceremony. A bell is blessed and then presented to the bride and groom by the officiant. The couple is then asked to give the bell a good hardy ring, while thinking lovingly of each other and, most importantly, of their future together.

The bell is then kept at home as a reminder of the couple's wedding day. When arguments arise, the bell is put to its intended use. One of the quarreling couple should ring the bell to call a truce in the argument. The tinkling sound will remind the couple of their wedding vows and conjure up the happiest memories from their wedding day.

The bell of truce originates from peasant traditions in the west of Ireland, and may well be derived from St. Patrick's Bell of Will. St. Patrick would often use bells in his ministrations and believed they would help him in performing miracles. He is said to have been buried with the Bell of Will, which was later exhumed and today is on display in Ireland's National Museum.

Many Irish crystal companies produce lovely hand-blown and hand-cut glass bells that may be used as a bell of truce. Pewter or iron bells may also be used, which would be more authentic, as St. Patrick's bell was crafted in iron.

# St. Brigid's Cross

ST. BRIGID'S DAY, February 1, is a saint's day celebrated all over Ireland. Brigid was born in 452 and was
baptized by St. Patrick. She entered the religious life and started the first community of
nuns in Ireland. Many miracles are attributed to Brigid, including changing
water into beer and making an
abundance of food out of little.

Brigid was the patron saint to the Knights of
Chivalry, and legend has it that the knights began
the custom of calling the girls they married
"brides" after St. Brigid.

Brigid is known as the patron saint of protection, and St.
Brigid's crosses are put up in homes all around Ireland to
invoke such protection. It is believed that Brigid converted a
pagan to Christianity on his deathbed by plaiting rushes she
found near the dying man's bed into the shape of the Cross
of Calvary.

When hung in the home, St. Brigid's crosses are thought
to protect a house against fire and the elements, as well as to
protect the occupants from sickness and disease. Many
believe that the cross also keeps out all evil spirits.

In many parts of Ireland newly married couples are presented with a St. Brigid's cross for their new homes and
then add a new one every year they live there. This custom

can begin at the wedding. Present the bride and groom with
a cross, along with this blessing:

*May St. Brigid bless and protect this cross,*
*the home where it rests, and the family who*
*gazes upon it.*

The cross should be presented by the bride's and groom's
mothers, since mothers have always been associated with
the home. This could be thought of as the last act of mother-
hood, offering protection to one's child as he or she enters
into a new life.

## A Celtic Offertory

THE ANCIENT CELTS would offer gifts to God on feast
days and during religious ceremonies. Many artifacts have
been unearthed at religious sites in Ireland that were thought
to be offerings to God. An offertory can be included as part
of the wedding ceremony, as a traditional means of giving
thanks to God for the new life a couple is about to enter.

If you are having a ceremony that includes communion,
the following Celtic offertory prayer can be recited by those
presenting bread and wine at the altar. This offertory prayer
was written by Rev. Cait Finnegan of the St. Ciaran's
Community.

*We bring bread and wine, symbolic of life,*
*that is shared out of Love, the new sacrifice.*
*And we offer to You, O God of our clan,*
*each thought word and deed, of each woman and man.*
*And with all creation, we raise up our prayers*
*O Christ our salvation, take our joys and our cares.*
*And the fire that lights the altar we dress*
*both warms us and guides us as we praise and bless.*
*And blessed holy water that mingles with wine,*
*a symbol of life, that brings life divine.*
*And once we have eaten this meal that we share,*
*Christ be our vision we see everywhere.*
*Christ be our neighbor, Christ be our heart.*
*Christ be in our loved ones, both near and apart.*
*Christ be our intention as we kiss in peace,*
*Christ be in our wills, let all warring cease.*
*Christ be on this altar now, in bread and wine,*
*as we share together in this sacred sign.*

# Irish Wedding Blessings

THERE ARE MANY different Irish wedding blessings that can be a part of your ceremony. Here are three of the most beautiful.

# IRISH WEDDING BLESSING I

May the road rise to meet you.
May the wind be always at your back.
May the sun shine warm upon your face,
The rains fall soft upon your fields.

May the light of friendship guide your paths together.
May the laughter of children grace the halls of your home.
May the joy of living for each other
trip a smile from your lips, a twinkle from your eye.

And when eternity beckons,
at the end of a life heaped high with love,
May the good Lord embrace you
with the arms that have nurtured you
the whole length of your joy-filled days.

May the gracious God hold you both
in the palm of His hands.
And, today, may the Spirit of Love
find a dwelling place in your hearts.

# IRISH WEDDING BLESSING II

*May joy and peace surround you both,*
*Contentment latch your door.*
*And happiness be with you now*
*And God bless you evermore.*

*May you live your life with trust,*
*And nurture your affection.*
*May your lifelong dreams*
*Come true for you,*
*Moving ever that direction.*

# IRISH WEDDING BLESSING III
## "OUR OWN" BY CAIT FINNEGAN

*Lord Jesus, bless our family*
*As we gather here today.*
*We have come to Your house together,*
*To celebrate and pray.*
*You've blessed us through the years Lord,*
*As we've lived with our joys and pains.*
*We give thanks for the love of each other*
*And we pass it on again.*

*We thank you for our faith Lord,*
*and the heritage we bear.*
*Let us pass to our sons and daughters,*
*this richness that we share.*

For though we are first generation,
or second, or third, or more;
We carry the pride and tradition
of those who first came to this shore.

So today as we honor love Lord,
we ask blessing on our own.
Let us learn from their many years, Lord,
to hold sacred our family and home.
For their marriage pays homage to You, Lord,
as does love for their family and friends.
Bless our joy as we share in this day Lord,
let this love we share never end.

# The First to Kiss the Bride

IRISH COUNTRY PEASANTS had many strong superstitions, and weddings were not exempt. It is deemed
appropriate that a man should always be the first to offer
best wishes and congratulations to the bride. Years of bad
luck would ensue if a woman were the first to wish joy, and
there are stories of jealous young girls grabbing hold of a
new bride to offer up the first unlucky kiss.

A pleasant way to preclude any bad luck would be to
include a first salutation in the wedding ceremony. After the
vows and exchange of rings, a male guest would be asked by

the officiant to come up and offer the first congratulations to the bride. This would be a wonderful way to include a special friend or family member in the wedding. The salutation could include an Irish blessing or perhaps a few heartfelt words from the participant, who would be wishing good luck and joy on behalf of all the guests in attendance.

## Coins and Confetti

IN LIMERICK, DURING the early part of the twentieth century, children would wait outside churches when weddings were in progress to "scramble for the coins." Coins would be mixed with confetti and rice and thrown as the bride and groom left the church after the ceremony.

This practice most likely derived from a nineteenth-century custom mentioned in *Ireland, Its Scenery, Character etc.*, a diary of the travels of Mr. and Mrs. S. C. Hall. Newly married grooms would give money to the poor who would be waiting along the roads after the wedding service. Here again we see an Irish superstition in practice, for it was believed that not giving to the poor would ensure bad luck in the marriage.

You can re-create this custom by having Irish pence on hand for the bride and groom to throw to guests as they leave the church. Another variation of this custom would be to hand out pouches to guests filled with Irish pence mixed with confetti, instead of rice or birdseed, which is popular to throw at weddings today. You can also fill the pouches with chocolate coins instead of real coins, which are lighter and not likely to give the bridal couple a concussion if they are accidentally hit on the head!

An even nicer way to honor this tradition, especially to ward off bad luck, would be to drop a check in the mail to your favorite charity on the morning of your wedding. A donation card can be given to your new spouse with an explanation that the donation ensures good luck for the marriage.

# Chapter Four

# TO THE CEILI

## The Irish Wedding Reception

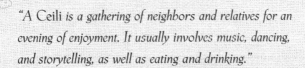

*"A Ceili is a gathering of neighbors and relatives for an evening of enjoyment. It usually involves music, dancing, and storytelling, as well as eating and drinking."*

SO IT IS NOTED IN *Field and Shore*, an anthology of daily life and traditions on the Aran Islands. A wedding in the family is the occasion most often associated with *ceilis* on the Aran Islands.

Hospitality is extremely important to the Irish. This has been true since ancient times in Ireland, when according to brehon laws, hospitality was considered the duty of each individual. It was considered a crime not to offer food and drink to any person who came to visit or who was passing in their travels.

This was still true in the nineteenth century. Wedding parties were usually simple affairs held at the home of the bride or groom, sometimes in the barn or outdoors if weather permitted. Having an ample supply of food and drink was deemed essential, or the family throwing the party would be thought of as extremely rude by the community and would most likely be slighted at future social events.

Wedding receptions in modern-day Ireland, as elsewhere, have become quite formal. They usually begin in the late afternoon after the ceremony with what is known as the sherry hour, when guests have a celebratory drink before going into a formal sit-down dinner. After dinner, often a five-course affair, there is music and dancing, the cake cutting, and plenty of time for "speeches," when family and friends rise to toast the bride and groom.

Very often additional guests, who have what is known as an "evening invitation," will then join the party. This custom came about in response to the high cost of weddings. Couples naturally want to include the many hometown friends that they've perhaps known for a lifetime, and the evening invitation is an economical way to do so. The party then continues with more dancing and drinking, and a late-night meal of sandwiches is often served. Irish weddings are known to go into the wee hours and sometimes continue until sunrise.

This chapter will present everything needed to throw a wedding reception with the feeling of an authentic Irish *ceili*. Included here are recipes for Irish food, suggestions for Irish drink, and some Irish toasts. Also, a discussion of Irish music, along with some decorating ideas and several amusing customs that should help make for an event that is "good craic"—an Irish expression meaning to have a good laugh and a great bit of fun.

# The Sherry Hour

IN MANY PARTS of Ireland the beginning of a wedding reception has come to be known as the sherry hour. This is a time for the guests to mingle and have a drink before going in to dinner. Often the wedding party is off being photographed and doesn't arrive until the end of the sherry hour.

Very little sherry is actually consumed during this cock-tail hour. Most guests opt for whiskey, a pint of beer, or a mixed drink. Here are some suggestions for drinks to serve during the sherry hour.

## IRISH WHISKEY IMPORTED FROM IRELAND

Jamesons

Bushmills Black Bush

John Power

Bushmills

Tullamore Dew

Middleton Rare

## IRISH WHISKEY AVAILABLE IN IRELAND (CALL THE IRISH RELATIVES!)

Paddy

Tyrconnell

Jameson Distillery Reserve

Red Breast

Kilbeggan

Coleraine

Irish whiskey was originally made by monks in sixth-century Ireland, who gave it the name *uisce beatha*, which translates as "the water of life."

With all the fantastic brands available, you may want to have a tasting menu of whiskeys to start off the reception. Have waiters pass trays of different brands so that guests may try a variety. Using stemmed or cordial glasses for sherry or port instead of a whiskey shot glass will add some elegance to this tasting menu. And keep in mind that Irish whiskey is traditionally served neat.

Not everyone will want to indulge in a whiskey, so chilled vodka, which comes in a variety of flavors, may also be served. Give the vodka an Irish touch by floating a shamrock in each glass, or use pansies, a flower indigenous to Ireland. A tray of sherry glasses floating with colorful pansies is a beautiful sight and a lovely way to begin the reception.

## IRISH BEERS, STOUTS, AND ALES

| | |
|---|---|
| Guinness Stout | Beamish Irish Stout |
| Harp Lager | Killian's Red |
| Smithwick's Ale | Kilkenny's Cream Ale |

Walk into any pub and ask for "a pint" and you will be given a glass of Guinness stout. Some call Guinness the national drink of Ireland, and it may be one of the country's oldest. Arthur Guinness took over a small brewery on the outskirts of Dublin in 1759. Local lore has it that he took a nine-hundred-year lease on the property at an annual rent of only £45 per year and has been brewing beer ever since.

There is much dispute about whether you can get a proper pint of Guinness off Irish soil. The Guinness company has introduced a floating draught system in its cans of beer that produces a smoother, creamier taste. A ball floats inside the can, which releases the recommended mix of $CO_2$ and nitrogen. A couple should now feel confident that an authentic-tasting Guinness can be served at their wedding reception for any relatives who may come over!

Harp is another popular beer in Ireland for those who would like something lighter than a stout. Pouring a "half and half"—half Guinness and half lager—or a "Black and Tan"—

half Guinness and half an amber beer like Killian's Red—
would be another option. To make a proper Black and Tan,
fill a pint halfway with an amber beer and then pour the
Guinness into the glass slowly over a spoon. The Guinness
will float on the top of the amber beer, creating the black and
tan look.

Here are some festive cocktails that can be served during
the sherry hour.

## The Irish Spring

1 oz. Irish whiskey

1 oz. orange juice

½ oz. raspberry liqueur

1 oz. sour mix

Serve on the rocks, garnished with an orange slice and a
cherry.

## A Black Irish

3 oz. Irish whiskey

1 oz. Kahlua

Serve on the rocks, garnished with cherries.

# An Emerald Martini

1½ oz. vodka or gin

1 splash Chartreuse

½ oz. dry vermouth

Serve straight up or on the rocks, garnished with a twist of lemon.

# An Irish Dog

2 oz. vodka

2 oz. Irish cream

Serve in a sherry glass or on the rocks.

# An Irish Highball

2 oz. Irish whiskey

4 oz. ginger ale

Serve on the rocks.

# The Irish Flag

1 oz. green crème de menthe

1 oz. Brandy

1 oz. Irish cream

Serve layered in a sherry glass.

# An Irish Seaman

1 oz. Irish cream

1 oz. spiced rum

Serve in a port glass or shot glass.

# An Irish Lady

3 oz. champagne

1 oz. melon liqueur

1 oz. orange juice

Serve in a champagne flute, garnished with an orange slice.
The ingredients for the Irish Lady may also be used to make
an Irish Lady Champagne punch.

# Irish Lady
# Champagne Punch

1 bottle of very chilled champagne

5 oz. orange juice, plus one tray of ice cubes made with
orange juice

4 oz. melon liqueur

1 thinly sliced orange for garnish

Add the first three ingredients to a chilled punch bowl and
float the orange slices on top. Ginger ale may be substituted
for the champagne, if you would like to make a nonalcoholic
punch.

# An Irish Wedding Meal

THE IRISH HAVE a strong connection with the food they eat. When one thinks of Irish cuisine, the first thing that comes to mind are hearty dishes with an emphasis on the potato, and it is true that in centuries past the Irish subsisted mainly on a diet of potatoes.

It is said that the average peasant family in the eighteenth century consumed about ten pounds of potatoes every day. Potatoes were easily grown in Ireland's mild, moist climate, which made them a mainstay of Irish diets. The Irish had become completely dependent on the potato by the mid 1800s and this dependence had a disastrous result. When the potato blight hit Ireland in 1845, over one million Irish died in the famine that followed.

But there is much more to Irish food than just the infamous potato. In recent years Ireland has had a great cuisine renaissance. Irish chefs like Margaret Johnson, Georgina Campbell, and Darina Allen, who have written some of Ireland's most popular Irish cuisine cookbooks, have rediscovered and reinvented classic Irish dishes that are unpretentious yet elegant.

Included here are dishes that would be appropriate to serve at a wedding reception from my own family's recipe box. Some have been passed through four generations of Irish women to my mother, Sara Margaret Beall. Sara Margaret has updated many of the oldest recipes, adding modern cooking techniques and ingredients to make them simpler to prepare today. She has included appetizers, soups, and main courses—everything for an authentic Irish wedding meal.

# Doolin Tart

*This recipe has been adapted from a classic meat-pie recipe and was named after the small village in County Clare. Doolin is on the west coast of Ireland and is the home of some of the greatest Irish musicians in the world. Doolin farmers will often carry meat pies out to the fields for their lunches.*

*Sara Margaret uses the Doolin meat-pie filling in delicate tart shells for an elegant yet hardy hors d'oeuvre. The white pudding, an Irish spiced pork sausage available in Irish specialty shops or by mail order, adds a nice flavor to the lamb.*

1 tablespoon butter

1 small yellow onion

1 pound ground lamb

8 ounces white pudding

40 1½-inch diameter frozen ready-to-bake mini pastry tart shells

Melt the butter in a medium-size skillet. Peel and finely mince the yellow onion and sauté it in the butter until barely translucent. Add the ground lamb and cook until lightly browned. Pour off grease and set aside.

In another skillet, crumble the white pudding and cook over high heat until browned. Add to lamb, mixing well.

Fill the tart shells with approximately 1 ounce of the lamb filling and bake shells according to package directions. Serve hot.

*Makes 40 mini tarts.*

# Shrove Pancakes with Caviar

*As a child, Sara Margaret looked forward to the beginning of Lent, when she was allowed to eat pancakes for dinner made from this simple Shrovetide recipe. For this appetizer, most of the sugar has been taken out of the family pancake recipe, so it won't compete with the salty caviar.*

3 eggs

1 cup flour

2 cups milk

1 teaspoon sugar

½ teaspoon salt

1 tablespoon butter, melted

Vegetable oil

½ cup sour cream

2 ounces of the best caviar you can afford

In a large bowl, beat eggs until bubbly. Add the next five ingredients and beat until a smooth batter forms. Coat a skillet with cooking oil. Using a tablespoon, drop a small amount of pancake batter on the heated skillet, forming pancakes that are about 2 inches across. Flip the pancakes when bubbles form.

Move pancakes to plate when cooked and let cool completely. When ready to serve, top pancakes with a small dab of sour cream and garnish with caviar.

*Makes 24 mini pancakes.*

# Angels on Horseback

*There are many versions of this rich appetizer that feature oysters as the main ingredient. Substituting sea scallops makes it easier to serve as a passing hors d'oeuvre. The Irish bacon this recipe calls for is much leaner than American-style bacon, but still has immense flavor. Adjust the quantities as needed, but plan on at least two per person—this one goes quickly.*

Sea scallops

Flour for dusting

Butter

Fresh lemon

Irish bacon

Toothpicks

Dip sea scallops in flour, completely covering in a light dusting. Melt a generous knob of butter in a pan on high heat. Quickly sauté the scallops on both sides until just browned, approximately 1 minute on each side. This will firm up the scallop and bring out its flavor. Let the scallops cool. Squeeze fresh lemon on the scallops.

Cut bacon into 4- to 5-inch-long pieces, depending on the size of the scallops. The bacon slice should be long enough to wrap around an entire scallop. Use a toothpick to secure one slice of bacon around each scallop.

Place the wrapped scallops on a cookie sheet and slide under a hot broiler. Cook about 7 minutes, turning the scallop halfway through so both sides of the bacon cook. Serve immediately.

# Irish Flag Terrine

*When this terrine is released from its mold, it has the look of the Irish tricolor. Garnish the serving plate with fresh cut shamrocks, if available.*

2 8-ounce packages cream cheese, softened

2 tablespoons finely diced roasted red peppers

Red, yellow, and green food coloring

4 ounces of goat cheese

1 white onion, finely chopped

1 tablespoon pesto sauce

To prepare the pan: Use a mini loaf pan, approximately 5¾ by 3¼ inches. Fold sheets of tinfoil to make two dividers, 3¼ inches wide by 4 inches tall. The foil dividers should be thick enough to stand when placed in pan.

Divide the cream cheese among three mixing bowls. To the first bowl add the roasted peppers with two drops of red food coloring and three drops of yellow food coloring. Beat with an electric mixer until you have a creamy orange color.

Place a piece of plastic wrap inside the loaf pan, so that the plastic hangs out generously on all four sides. Place a divider one-third of the way along the length of the pan. Fill the divided section with the red pepper mixture. Place the pan in the freezer for about 20 minutes to set.

Meanwhile, in the second bowl, mix the goat cheese and chopped onion with the cream cheese, using the electric mixer. Be sure to clean the beaters before you use them, to remove any orange residue.

Remove the loaf pan from the freezer and place the second divider two-thirds of the way along the length of the pan. You should now have three equal sections for each cheese. Pour the goat cheese mixture into the middle section and place in the freezer for 15 minutes to set.

Using the electric mixer, blend the premade pesto and three drops of green food coloring into the third bowl of cream cheese. Remove the chilled loaf pan from the freezer and place the pesto mixture into the remaining third of the pan.

Chill an additional 20 minutes. Remove the loaf pan from the freezer and gently remove the dividers. Chill for an additional 24 hours in the refrigerator.

When ready to serve, gently flip the loaf pan onto a plate. Remove the pan and plastic. Serve with assorted crackers.

*Serves 8–10 as an appetizer.*

# Seafood Broth

This soup has many of the same ingredients as a seafood chowder. Heavy cream is whipped and added at the very end to give the soup a creamy flavor without making the broth milky. Any type of fish or shellfish may be used. Seafood Broth will serve at least twelve people as a first course.

This recipe originated from a pub in Roundstone, a lovely fishing village on the coast of Connemara, County Galway.

8 cups fish stock

2 cups chicken stock

12 baby new potatoes, scrubbed and quartered

2 small onions, finely chopped

1 clove garlic, minced

5 celery stalks, chopped

3 carrots, chopped

4 tablespoons butter

1 bay leaf

1 dozen mussels

1 dozen littleneck clams

¾ pound fresh salmon

¾ pound fresh haddock or sole

¾ pound bay scallops

1 dozen medium-sized shrimp

1 dozen oysters, shucked

6 sprigs of fresh dill

½ pint heavy whipping cream

Fresh chives, snipped, for garnish

In a heavy stock pot, add fish stock, chicken stock, potatoes, onions, garlic, celery, carrots, butter, and bay leaf. Boil on high heat for about 15 minutes, until the potatoes are just tender. Turn down heat so the broth slowly simmers.

While the stock is boiling, steam mussels and clams in a separate pot until shells open. Discard any unopened shells. Remove the mussels and clams from their shells and add to the stock pot.

Cut the raw salmon and white fish into bite-size chunks, removing any skin. Add to the stock pot. Add the rest of the fish, shellfish, and the dill sprigs. Cover pot and let simmer for 1 hour.

When ready to serve soup, whip the heavy cream, using an electric beater until stiff peaks form. Ladle soup into serving bowls and add a heaping teaspoon of the whipped cream. Sprinkle with fresh chives, if handy.

*Serves 12*

# Ceili Chicken

*This dish was originally called Gaelic Chicken by Mary David McFaddin, my grandmother, but Sara Margaret adopted the title "Ceili Chicken" when she began serving it at parties. Ceili Chicken has similar ingredients to the classic Irish dish Gaelic Steak.*

¾ cup (12 tablespoons) butter

1 large onion, finely chopped

1 clove garlic, minced

3 tablespoons flour

2 14½-ounce cans chicken broth

½ teaspoon salt

2 pinches nutmeg

¼ cup Irish whiskey, plus 1 tablespoon, if desired

1 cup heavy cream

6 boneless, skinless chicken breasts

Flour, for dusting

24 button mushrooms, washed and stemmed

½ cup chopped fresh chives

Melt ½ cup of the butter in a saucepan and sauté onion and garlic until transparent. Add flour to thicken. Blend in chicken broth and season with salt and nutmeg. Add the ¼ cup whiskey and the cream. Allow to simmer slowly for about 30 minutes. Add the 1 tablespoon whiskey to flavor, if desired, and allow to simmer 10–15 minutes more until sauce is thickened.

While sauce is simmering, dust chicken breasts in flour. Melt remaining ¼ cup of butter and sauté chicken until browned on both sides and almost cooked, about 3–5 minutes per side.

Transfer chicken breasts to baking pan. Place mushroom caps on top of chicken breasts and pour sauce over chicken and mushrooms. Sprinkle chives over all. Cover baking pan with foil and bake at 325 degrees until hot, about 35–40 minutes. Keep chicken warm at 200 degrees until ready to serve.

*Serves 8–10 people.*

# Wild Berry Lamb

*This lamb dish is wonderful during the summer when fresh blackberries are available. It is also possible to get excellent frozen Marion berries, a sweet variety of blackberry, so this dish can be made year-round. Using a leg of lamb instead of a rack of lamb will keep the cost down for a wedding reception.*

1 6-pound leg of lamb

12 1-inch-long fresh rosemary sprigs, plus 4 long sprigs

Olive oil for drizzling

Salt and pepper

Preheat the oven to 425 degrees. Trim the excess fat off the leg of lamb and place in a shallow baking pan. Make twelve small incisions into the lamb with a sharp knife and insert the 1-inch sprigs of rosemary. Lay the long sprigs of rosemary on top of the lamb and drizzle with olive oil so they won't dry out. Lightly salt and pepper.

Turn down the oven to 350 degrees and place the leg of lamb on the middle rack. Cook about 20 minutes per pound for medium-rare lamb. The meat thermometer should read 150 degrees. Let the lamb rest, covered with tinfoil, for 10 minutes before carving.

## WILD BLACKBERRY SAUCE

2 cups fresh blackberries or frozen Marion berries

1 cup port wine

1 cup water

2 tablespoons sugar, or to taste

2 cinnamon sticks

4 sprigs fresh thyme

½ teaspoon black pepper

Reserve a few whole berries to garnish the lamb, then place all ingredients in a saucepan and simmer on low heat until the liquid is reduced by ⅓ and the berries are tender. Add more sugar, if desired, to taste. Remove thyme sprigs and cinnamon sticks and purée sauce in a blender.

Strain to remove seeds. Keep berry sauce covered until lamb is ready and serve warm. Place a few fresh blackberries next to the lamb and ladle sauce over the berries. Do not cover lamb with sauce, as it can be too sweet.

*Serves 8–10 people.*

# The Salmon of Knowledge

SALMON HAS THE distinction of being the subject of one of Ireland's best-known Celtic myths. When serving it at an Irish wedding reception, be sure to tell guests this story, retold in *Heroes of the Dawn* edited by Duncan Baird, of the Salmon of Knowledge.

At the source of the Boyne River there were hazel trees on which grew nuts filled with great wisdom. A strong breeze blew one day and dropped the wise nuts into the river, where they were eaten by a salmon. It was deemed that the first person to eat the salmon would gain all the world's wisdom.

Finnegas, a bard, caught the salmon and had his apprentice, Finn MacCool, cook it over a fire. While the salmon cooked, a blister rose on its skin. Finn poked the blister with this thumb and in doing so scalded himself. He sucked the thumb to ease the pain and tasted the flesh of the salmon. Thus Finn MacCool gained eternal wisdom.

## Baked Salmon

*This is a baked salmon recipe that can be served hot or cold. The mayonnaise in the recipe keeps the salmon moist and flavorful so that it doesn't need an additional sauce.*

1 large (about 5–6 pounds) salmon fillet

1 cup mayonnaise

2 bunches fresh dill

3 or 4 lemons

2 small yellow onions

½ cup white wine

Place a long sheet of tinfoil in a shallow baking dish, using enough so that the foil can be closed up, creating a pocket for the salmon. Place the salmon fillet in the center of the baking dish on the tinfoil.

Cover the entire fillet with a light coating of mayonnaise. Snip one bunch of the fresh dill over the entire fillet and squeeze one of the lemons over as well. Thinly slice the other lemons and lay the slices over the fillet.

Slice the onion in paper–thin slices and lay them on top of the lemon. Add a final layer of dill sprigs. Lightly sprinkle the wine over the salmon, using care not to wash off the layer of dill, lemon, and onions.

Close the foil around the salmon, creating a foil pocket. Bake in a hot 350 degree oven until the salmon is flaky. Check the salmon at 30 minutes; then watch closely. Serve hot or cold with additional lemon slices.

*Serves 6 people.*

# Champ

*No Irish wedding reception meal would be complete without a potato dish served with the main course. Champ is mashed potatoes mixed with green onions and milk or cream.*

*The traditional way to eat champ is with a well of melted butter in the middle of the mound of potatoes, so that you can dip each spoonful of potato into the melted butter. It would be difficult to do this for a large number of guests at a wedding reception, so this recipe includes the butter blended in with the potatoes.*

6 large potatoes, peeled and diced

1 cup heavy cream

3 bunches green onions, finely chopped

1 stick (8 tablespoons) butter

Salt and pepper to taste

Put the diced potatoes in a large pan of salted water and boil until soft, about 20 minutes. Drain the water and set the potatoes aside. Pour the heavy cream into a saucepan and add the chopped green onions. Let simmer on stovetop until both the white and green part of the onion is tender, about 5 minutes.

Mash the potatoes by hand, adding the stick of butter, a tablespoon or two at a time.

When onions are tender, remove them from the heavy cream with a slotted spoon and add to the potatoes. Add ¼ cup of the hot cream to the potatoes and blend with an electric mixer until potatoes are smooth. Serve potatoes with steamed carrots and green beans, for a plate with some Irish color.

*Serves 8–10.*

# Irish Brown Bread

*Irish Brown Bread, a coarse whole-grain bread, is a staple of the Irish diet and is served at most every table in Ireland. This recipe and the one on the next page, for Irish Soda Bread, come from the Traditional Irish Bakery, an Irish bakery and retail food shop located in the heart of New York City's immigrant Irish community.*

> 4 cups stone-ground whole-wheat flour
>
> 4 cups bread flour
>
> 3 teaspoons salt
>
> 2 teaspoons baking soda
>
> 3–4 cups low-fat cultured buttermilk

Mix all the dry ingredients together in a large bowl. Make a well in the center and add some buttermilk. Work the mixture with your hands until the dough is soft but not too sticky. On a floured board, turn out the dough and knead into a disk about three inches thick.

Place in a very hot preheated oven, 475 degrees, for 20 minutes. Turn the oven down to 400 degrees and bake for another 20 minutes. Bread should sound hollow when you tap the loaf on its back.

*Makes 1 loaf.*

# Irish Soda Bread

*Irish Soda Bread is a favorite at Irish American tables. The Traditional Irish Bakery recommends putting a loaf of soda bread and a loaf of Irish brown bread in a basket for each table at the wedding reception.*

3 cups flour

1 teaspoon baking soda

1 teaspoon baking powder

2 teaspoons sugar

1 cup raisins

1 cup buttermilk

Sift the flour, baking soda, and baking powder into a bowl. Add the sugar and raisins. Stir with a wooden spoon to mix. Add the buttermilk and form a dough. On a floured surface, knead dough by continuously folding the dough into itself.

Form dough into a round loaf and cut a cross on the top of the dough to keep the bread from bursting during the baking. Bake for 35–40 minutes at 350 degrees.

*Makes 1 loaf*

# The Irish Wedding Cake

A TRADITIONAL IRISH wedding cake is very different from the wedding cakes in the United States. Irish wedding cake is a rich fruitcake filled with raisins, currants, cherries, dates, and sliced almonds. It is often infused with brandy or Irish whiskey, depending on the recipe.

The cake is made about three months before the wedding and stored in airtight tins, to let the liquor fully infuse into the cake. A week before the wedding, the tins are opened and a layer of almond icing, very similar to marzipan, is spread over the cake. This almond layer is applied before the cake is iced and allowed to dry completely to form a support for the royal icing.

Very often a member of the family or a special friend who has a knack for it will offer to make a couple's wedding cake. Cake recipes are often a guarded secret passed down from mother to daughter. Sometimes a cake will be made at home and then taken to a professional baker to be iced. Most bakeries in Ireland will ice homemade cakes as they appreciate the importance of a family recipe.

There is some lovely symbolism in the Irish wedding cake. The richness of the cake is thought to offer a promise of prosperity for the couple, as well as representing fertility, for a wealth of children.

When the cake is cut and shared with guests, the bride and groom are thought to be sharing their prosperity and happiness. Because the rich fruitcake keeps well for weeks, pieces of wedding cake are often sent to friends who cannot attend the wedding. This is another way for the newly married bride and groom to spread their wealth and euphoria.

The following cake recipe is from Cakes and Company, Ireland's premier wedding cake designers. If you are planning to serve this traditional wedding cake, you should serve what the Irish call a "finger slice," a slice of cake that is no wider than a finger, because of its richness.

It you decide to have a layer cake, you can still have a smaller version of the Irish wedding cake on hand for guests to try. If you do use the traditional fruitcake recipe, be sure to save the top layer, well wrapped and stored in a freezer. The Irish serve this top layer at their first child's christening.

Decorations for any cake you choose may include shamrocks, designs from Celtic art, or maybe a heraldic harp, Celtic cross, or Irish flag.

# Irish Wedding Cake

4 cups currants

1 cup sultanas (golden raisins)

1 cup raisins

¾ cup glacéed cherries, finely chopped

2 cups orange juice or brandy

1½ cups white flour

¼ teaspoon salt

¼ teaspoon ground nutmeg

½ teaspoon allspice

1½ cups (3 sticks) unsalted butter

1½ cups brown sugar

4 eggs

¼ cup slivered almonds

1 teaspoon molasses

Grated rind of 1 lemon

Grated rind of 1 orange

Soak the first four ingredients in orange juice or brandy overnight.

Preheat the oven to 275 degrees. Grease an 8-inch round or 7-inch square cake pan and line with waxed paper.

Sift flour, salt, and spices into a large mixing bowl. In another bowl cream the butter and sugar until the mixture is fluffy and light.

Beat the eggs in a separate bowl and then gradually add them to the creamed mixture. Beat thoroughly after each addition. Fold in the flour and spices. Stir in the soaked fruit with any liquid, almonds, molasses, and the grated orange and lemon rinds. Spoon the mixture into the prepared cake pan, spreading it out evenly with the back of a spoon.

Tie a piece of brown paper around the outside of the pan. The brown paper keeps the cake from overbrowning on the outside, allowing the cake to cook through. Cover the top of the cake with 2 sheets of waxed paper cut to fit. Make a hole in the center of the paper, about the size of a quarter.

Put the cake on the lower shelf of the oven and let it bake without opening the door. It will most likely take 5 to 5½ hours to bake, but check the cake after 4½ hours.

When the cake is done, remove from oven and let cool completely. Sprinkle lightly with brandy or Irish whiskey. Wrap the cake in waxed paper and plastic wrap and store in an airtight container.

Ideally the cake should be baked and stored three months in advance. Whiskey or brandy should be sprinkled on the cake two additional times, but very lightly, so the cake does not get too wet.

About a week before the wedding, the cake should be iced with almond icing or a layer of marzipan. Let the cake stand for 24 to 48 hours, until completely dry. Then ice and decorate with royal icing or almond paste.

To make additional tiers of the cake, double the ingredients for a 10-inch pan, and double again for a 12-inch pan. Allow additional baking time for larger pans. The time will depend on the oven, but it could be as much as double for the largest pan. Cake is done when an inserted toothpick comes out clean.

*Serves 125*

# Irish Decor

WHETHER THE RECEPTION is a small intimate dinner for thirty or a ballroom affair for three hundred, there are many ways to add an Irish flair to the decor. The Irish symbols discussed in chapter 2 can play an integral part in the decoration for the reception. Here are some suggestions inspired by Irish history, Celtic myths, and the symbols associated with Ireland.

## THE CENTERPIECE

The reception tables are perhaps the best place to add some Irish-inspired decorations. Try one of these ideas.

*Irish Crystal, Lace, and Linen*—Cover tables with pieces of Irish lace or linen. Place crystal vases and bowls filled with flowers indigenous to Ireland in the center of each table. While authentic Irish linen, lace, and crystal can be expensive, you can also achieve the same look with items bought at discount glassware and fabric stores.

*The May Bush*—The Irish version of a Maypole, May bushes were presented to newly married couples in ancient Ireland. Small topiary trees decorated with streaming ribbons, brightly colored paper, and golden balls can be placed on reception tables. Use a tent card to describe the history of the May bush, so guests can appreciate this Irish tradition.

*Aengus and Caer, a Celtic Myth*—Aengus Og is known as the God of Love, and the story of Aengus and Caer is the most romantic in all of Celtic mythology. Aengus dreamed of Caer, a beautiful gentlewoman who lived near a lake. He traveled many miles to find Caer and pledge his love to her. When he arrived at the lake, Aengus found that Caer had taken the form of a swan. Aengus then pledged his eternal love to Caer by transforming himself into a swan so they would be together forever.

This Celtic tale of swans in love can be portrayed in an elegant yet simple centerpiece. Lay a round or oval mirror flat on the table to represent water. Surround the mirror with greenery and flowers, creating a delicate lakelike setting. Place two crystal or china swans on the mirror to represent the swan lovers Aengus and Caer.

*A Centerpiece of Celtic Herbs*—Let the Celtic love of nature and the outdoors be an inspiration for this centerpiece. In woven baskets, place the following fruits, plants, and herbs, which the Celts believed had special powers: The colorful anemone flowers were believed to be adored by fairies, who would nestle in them at night. Yarrow and purple orchids were two herbal blossoms used as love charms. Celtic bridesmaids brought yarrow to weddings to create seven years of love. Ivy, marigolds, and juniper berries were thought to offer protection. Hazelnuts brought great wisdom when eaten and were the most beloved of the *Sidhe*, the Irish underground fairies, as were apples, which are called the "fruit of life" by Irish fairies.

*Tir Na N'og, Land of the Fairies*—The Irish believe in a special world called Tir Na N'og, the Land of the Ever Young. This is a mystical place where Irish fairies live a life of luxurious comfort. By calling on the powers of the *Sidhe*, a wedding reception can be transformed into this sumptuous fairy kingdom.

Fairies love all things beautiful and opulent. Decorations for a fairy's banquet table might include pieces of colored glass, gold and silver decanters, and crystal bowls and goblets filled with jewels, including pearls, diamonds, and rubies. Anything that sparkles is coveted by the *Sidhe*. They love twinkling lights, which can be placed in strands around the room. Tinsel and glitter can embellish anything a fairy might touch. Fabrics of shimmering silver and spun gold are most desired by fairies and can be used to cover tables.

Fairies also love the color green, which represents the fields and forests that they roam. Foxglove, fuchsia, prim-rose, and shamrocks conceal the entrances to fairy forts and can be used to decorate the banquet tables.

There might even be a few fairies on hand to help serve the banquet: Fairy wings to adorn the attire of servers can be made or purchased.

## PLACE CARDS, FAVORS, AND NAPKINS

The shamrock, the harp, the Celtic cross, and familial coats of arms—these are all Irish emblems that can be inscribed on place cards, favor boxes, napkin rings, and even tented table numbers.

It is even possible to put an Irish design on the corner of fabric napkins. Copy your favorite Irish images on heat transfer paper and then iron them directly onto fabric. You may continue to use these napkins after the wedding recep-tion; the image will fade with washing, creating a beautiful patina on the napkin.

*Ogham Script*—Ogham was the first known writing in Ireland. This alphabet consists of a series of lines and notches placed in groups along a thicker baseline. Ogham dates back to the third century and can be found today on stone grave markers and memorials in southern Ireland. Ogham script is also known as the tree alphabet because each letter takes the name of an ancient tree. You can use Ogham script on place cards for the reception. Write the name of a guest on the place card and his name in Ogham script directly underneath. The Ogham alphabet can be found in Irish gift shops, and many sell Ogham-inscribed jewelry.

## PASSING TRAYS

Try adding an Irish flourish to the trays that are used to pass hors d'oeuvres. New York City event designer Amy Brentano suggests using gold- and silver-leafed picture frames as passing trays. Place a map of Ireland, a picture of the Irish countryside, some Irish lace, or a photograph of an Irish castle under the glass of the frame. Appetizers can then be placed on top of the glass and passed by waiters.

You can also make a tray that looks like a fairy forest by taking a piece of old weathered wood and embellishing it with rocks, moss, and maybe an Irish leprechaun. Place a piece of clean slate on top of the wood on which to set the hors d'oeuvres.

# Burning of the Turf

THE CUTTING OF turf for fuel is a tradition that has gone on in rural Ireland for centuries. Turf is cut from the boglands of Ireland, which currently cover one-sixth of the country. This is a tradition that was born out of necessity, as there are very few forests left in Ireland and coal is also scarce.

Peat, as it is also called, is the most ancient of Irish habitat, with some of the oldest bogland dating back more than ten thousand years. In County Mayo there have been discoveries of stone walls, houses, tools, and numerous tombs, long buried under ever-shifting layers of turf. Peasants believed that turf came out of the earth carrying the memories of ancestors from long ago.

To honor your Irish ancestors, build a turf fire if there is access to a fireplace at the reception site. The distinctive and pleasant smell of peat will delight any Irish relatives in attendance, reminding them of sitting by an open hearth with a cup of tea and the blue smoke of a turf fire.

If there is no access to a fireplace, small pieces of turf can be put on decorative tiles around the reception area and burned like incense. The scent will give the entire party a cozy feel. Peat can be found in Irish gift shops. It is also possible to order it on the Internet.

# A Celtic Pebble Tradition

THIS IS A custom that can be celebrated if the couple is having their reception near water. Couples in ancient Ireland were often married near a river, lake, or holy well. It was believed that these were sacred places favored by the Celtic gods. Wedding guests were given small stones or pebbles to cast into the water while making a wish for the couple's future happiness.

If a couple is having their reception near water, small cloth bags of pebbles can be presented to guests as they arrive at the reception to be used for wish making.

It is also possible to celebrate this tradition by setting up a large clear vase at a table next to a bowl of small river rocks. Guests can make a wish for the wedding couple as they pitch a rock into the vase. The couple can then save the vase, filled with their loved ones' best wishes, to use in their new home. Be sure to place a card with an explanation next to the vase, so guests will understand that their wishes are a contribution to the bride and groom's Irish heritage.

# Music for the Reception

IRISH MUSIC MAY be the most important aspect for a wedding reception reminiscent of an authentic *ceili*. For the

Irish, music infuses most every milestone of their lives, and there is a long tradition of celebrating a wedding with music as well as dancing.

The music at weddings was a simple affair in centuries past. Often a few musicians would be called on to play jigs, waltzes, and reels for dancing. These dance tunes have evolved into what is now called "traditional music" in Ireland. Traditional Irish music commonly employs these instruments:

*Fiddle*—The difference between a fiddle and a violin is attitude and technique!

*Uilleann Pipes*—A bagpipe developed in Ireland, thought to evolve from Irish war pipes in the beginning of the eighteenth century. Wisdom says that it takes seven years of practice and seven years of playing to make a piper.

*Flute and Tin Whistle*—Simple system versions of these instruments are played, often with the breath accentuated.

*Bodhran*—A shallow one-sided drum, usually made of goatskin.

*Concertina*—A small accordion-like instrument that blends well with the fiddle. Button accordions are also played.

These instruments are what you will hear if you go to a

"traditional session" in an Irish pub. The instruments were also used in groups known in the late twenties as *ceili* bands, bands that played for public dances.

According to Ciaran Carson in his book *Irish Traditional Music,* in the sixties, the *ceili* band evolved into the concept of group playing with a "solo effect." This was led by a man named Sean O'Riada who founded the group Ceoltoiri Cualann, which eventually evolved into the world–renowned group The Chieftains. O'Riada was on the fore-front of the "traditional music" revival, which has exploded in Ireland and around the world.

Today it is possible to find gifted Irish musicians in most communities. Having an Irish band play at the wedding reception will truly be the highlight of the day.

As mentioned previously, Irish musicians can be found through local Irish newspapers and through Irish organiza-tions such as the Ancient Order of Hibernians. Irish music has proliferated on the Internet as evidenced by the numer-ous websites devoted to traditional music, many of which include referrals to Irish bands for hire.

Irish recordings are an excellent option if an Irish band cannot be found locally, or if a couple does not want to devote the entire reception to Irish music.

Here are some suggestions for Irish musicians and bands who have recorded music that would be appropriate for the wedding reception.

| | |
|---|---|
| The Chieftains | The Wild Rovers |
| Celtic Thunder | Van Morrison |
| Gaelic Storm | Davy Spillane |
| Da Danaan | Black 47 |
| Clannad | Clancy Brothers |
| Waterboys | Loreena McKennett |
| Solnas | Altan |
| Christy Moore | Druid Stone |
| James Galway | Dolores Keane |
| U2 | Enya |
| The Three Irish Tenors | Elvis Costello |

There are also superb compilations of Irish music. Here are a few of the many excellent recordings that would add great fun to the wedding reception.

- *Wedding and Love Songs* (Claddagh/Atlantic)  Traditional as well as popular music for weddings.

- *Druid Stone: The Vow, an Irish Wedding Collection* (Northstar)  Excellent music for the dinner hour.

- *A Wedding Song Collection* (Rego)  Sentimental favorites.

- *Mighty Session* (Rego)  An excellent introduction to traditional music.

+ *New Irish Dance Party* (Rego)  Popular songs for Irish dancing.

+ *130 Irish Party Songs* (Rego)  A difinitive three–CD set of popular Irish songs.

+ *Songs of Ireland* (Rego)  The classic songs associated with the Irish.

+ *Celtic Love Songs* (Celtophile)  A lovely slow–tempo CD.

+ *Irish Heartbeat* (Uni/Poldor)  Van Morrison and the Chieftans present a rousing, joyous collection of Irish songs.

+ *In Ireland* (RCA)  James Galway and the Chieftains combine for a beautiful collection of traditional Irish music.

# The Strawboys

RURAL WEDDING PARTIES in the nineteenth century in both northern and southern Ireland would often include the antics of the strawboys, local lads who had not been invited to the festivities and who would show up dressed in hats and capes made of straw, hiding their appearance. In the course of their merrymaking, they would often insist on dancing with the bride. Even though they created a disturbance, it was considered good luck for the bride and groom if there were a visit from the strawboys.

Strawboys are still around in Ireland today. They are a regular feature at weddings on Achill Island. Eileen Reilly, an Irish Studies professor at New York University, had them at her recent wedding when she went home to marry in County Longford. She describes a group of men with tall, pointed straw hats hiding their faces, who arrived during her reception. They brought their own musicians and entertained the guests with Irish set dancing.

The strawboys are one of the most widely known of rural wedding customs. Numerous Irish history and folklore books mention a version of strawboys, soppers, or ragamuffins, so this would be a significant custom to re-create at your wedding. To surprise wedding guests, hire local Irish musicians to play during the reception. This is a good way to include some Irish music, especially if you are planning to have a more contemporary, non-Irish band play for the majority of the event.

If Irish musicians are hard to find, dress up a group of friends as strawboys and play some recorded Irish music, so they may keep up the tradition of dancing with the bride.

Strawboy hats can be made using straw and raffia found in craft stores. An easier way to have the essence of a strawboy is to ask the musicians or your friends to wear vests and caps decorated with straw. If possible, it would be nice to have at least one strawboy whose appearance is hidden.

To make a straw hood, based on the look of the original straw hoods worn by strawboys in Ireland, the supplies needed from a craft store are:

1 bag of natural raffia

1 12-inch-wide wooden embroidery hoop

3 32-inch-long decorative straw brooms

1. Wrap strands of raffia around the embroidery hoop until it is completely covered. Break apart the brooms and separate the sheaves of straw into bundles of 5 or 6.

2. Begin tying a bundle of sheaves to the hoop with raffia. Tie in the middle of the grain so there are a couple inches below the hoop and the stem extends above the hoop. Leave about an inch of space on the hoop between bundles and continue tying bundles until you have circled the hoop.

3. Grab hold of the top of each bundle of straw and tie them all together with raffia, creating a cone shape. Trim the straw at the top and the ends with scissors

for a clean look or leave the hat wild and unruly, like the strawboys themselves!

# The Cake Dance

THE CAKE DANCE is a festive custom sure to add lots of amusement to your wedding reception. Cake dances took place in Ireland on feast days and also at *ceilis*. A contest would often be held during the course of the dance, with couples competing for the grand prize of a home-baked cake. Easter was the most popular time for a cake dance and the expression "that takes the cake" comes from these Easter competitions.

At the wedding reception, announce a dance contest and ask couples to come on the dance floor and try some Irish step dancing. Hiring a group of step dancers to perform and help with the contest is one way to get the festivities going. The finest dancing couple will be awarded the grand prize, a miniature version of the wedding cake.

If there are going to be many young children at the wedding, the cake dance could be an event just for them or have a simpler event called a cake walk. Place squares decorated with different Irish symbols on the dance floor. These could include shamrocks, harps, and leprechauns, but one of the squares should be a picture of a wedding cake. As the music is played, the children begin walking around the squares.

When the music stops, the child who lands on the wedding cake takes home the prize.

## The Jaunting Char

THERE ARE MANY different types of dances in Ireland, some of which are formal and known as set dances. The jaunting char is a lively informal dance originally performed by young men in the west of Ireland. The groom is hoisted up on a chair by his "best lads" and presented to guests.

The jaunting char dance was most likely named after the horse-drawn jaunting carts found in places like the Aran Islands. These carts are fairly high above the ground and can give quite a bumpy ride—similar to that of a bunch of eager lads raising a mate above their heads for some joyous fun.

Care should be taken if the jaunting char is to be celebrated with a surprised groom at his wedding reception. Be sure to have at least two able-bodied men per chair leg. Using a sturdy wood chair is also a good idea, as collapsible folding chairs can be quite unstable. A rousing patriot march would be excellent music to play for the jaunting char.

# Irish Toasts

*Three glories of speech:*
*Steadiness—Wisdom—Brevity*

DURING WEDDING RECEPTIONS in Ireland a time is set aside for family and guests to offer up a toast to the bride and groom. Usually both the bride's and groom's father, the best man, and assorted friends, both male and female, will wish the couple well. The groom will also make a speech thanking everyone for coming and toasting his new bride.

Here are a handful of Irish toasts, selected from the hundreds that would be appropriate to offer up to the newlyweds. For some fun, ask each member of the wedding party to pick a toast and recite it during this time for speeches.

*May your thoughts be glad as the shamrocks.*
*May your heart be as light as a song.*
*May each day bring you bright happy hours,*
*That stay with you all year long.*
*For each petal on the shamrock,*
*This brings a wish your way.*
*Good health, good luck, and happiness,*
*For today and every day.*

May you have warm words on a cold evening,
A full moon on a dark night,
And a smooth road every time you take to home.

May you have—
Walls for the wind,
And a roof for the rain,
And drinks by the fire,
And all heart's desire,
And laughter to cheer you,
And those you love near you.

Good Times,
Good Friends,
Good Cheer to you;
And the luck of the Irish
In all that you do.

May the Strength of three be in your Journey.

Let's put on our dancing shoes,
And wear our shamrocks green,
And toast to friends both here and there,
And everywhere in-between.

*May flowers always line your path*
*And sunshine light your day,*
*May songbirds serenade you,*
*Every step along the way,*
*May a rainbow run beside you,*
*In a sky that's always blue,*
*And may happiness fill your heart,*
*Each day your whole life through.*

*May God grant you many years to live,*
*For sure he must be knowing,*
*The earth has angels all too few,*
*And heaven is overflowing.*

*May the sons of your sons fill your home with laughter.*

*May you both live as long as you want;*
*And never want as long as you live.*
*May we see your wrinkled hands combing your grandchild's*
*    hair.*
*And when you finally move on . . .*
*May you be in heaven half an hour before*
*the devil knows you're dead.*

*Irish Families are . . .*
*One of God's greatest treasures;*
*One of life's nicest pleasures.*
*A refuge in good times and bad . . .*
*A place of peace that you're happy to have.*
*Its members are always there,*
*With unconditional love to share.*
*So I raise a glass to this clan;*
*Long life, great love, and good health*
*To each child, woman, and man.*

## An Irish Song

THE CUSTOM OF clinking a glass with a spoon to get a couple to kiss has undergone a wonderful transition in Ireland. At a recent Irish wedding, guests were asked not to hit their glasses when they wanted the bridal couple to embrace, but instead to rise and sing a song with the word "love" in the lyrics.

To the couple's delight, many of their friends and family stood up to show off their beautiful singing voices. There are many Irish love songs that would be appropriate to use for this delightful custom—or perhaps guests could recite a favorite love poem, which may be more appropriate for bashful types who fear singing in public. Reciting a song or poem is in keeping with the *ceili* tradition and the Irish consider it a gift to offer up an eloquent performance.

## The Whiskey Walk

THIS TRADITION HAS been adopted in Ireland by young groomsmen in the Cork area. It seems to have its origins in an Asian wedding tradition.

Bottles of whiskey are put on each reception table. The groom then makes the rounds, being honored in a toast from each bottle by his friends at every table.

This can be an opportunity to showcase the many different Irish whiskeys available, putting a different brand at each table.

It is highly suggested that the groom pace himself, leaving plenty of time between toasts, so as not to become tipsy. Perhaps taking just a sip, instead of an entire shot, of whiskey is the remedy in this situation—although I'm told a groom would never get away with that in Cork!

# The Bride's Bottle

AFTER IRISH COUNTRY wedding ceremonies during the nineteenth and early twentieth centuries, there was much revelry and merrymaking during the journey home. Men would often race each other wildly on horses or engage in competitions of strength. The winner would receive a coveted bottle of whiskey from the hand of the bride, hence the name "Bride's Bottle."

A competition for the Bride's Bottle would be an amusing diversion for the reception or rehearsal dinner. Here are some ideas for amusements that don't rely on strength or endurance and include young and old alike.

+ Play twenty questions, the topic being trivia about the bride and groom.

+ Plan a scavenger hunt, sending the participants off to hunt for items from some of the bride and groom's favorite places.

+ Play charades with categories including the bride and groom's favorite books, music, movies, etc.

+ Plan an Irish cabaret competition. Guests are asked to sing an Irish song, dance a jig to Irish music, or recite some Irish poetry. To level the playing field and get those who don't feel they have performance skills to participate, choose the winner not by artistic merit but by the level of enthusiasm.

A nice bottle of Irish whiskey can be the grand prize for the Bride's Bottle competition, or you might perhaps give out mini whiskey bottles to all participating, so everyone is a winner.

# Irish Clay Pipes

AT WEDDINGS, WAKES, and other gatherings, long pipes made out of clay would be filled with tobacco and laid out on trays along with Irish whiskey. Clay pipes, which are also known as "dudeens," can be seen in many sketches and photographs of Irish life in the past three hundred years.

The pipes were made in Ireland, in the town of Knock-croghery, in County Roscommon, until the factory was burned down during the war for independence. Recently, at the site of the original factory, production of the pipes has begun again. Potters using the original pipe molds, tools, and methods are happily making these "instruments of leisure."

Cigar smoking has again become an accepted activity at celebrations like weddings. Having Irish clay pipes on hand will be an amusing diversion for cigar and pipe smokers alike.

# Jumping the Fire

DURING THE HEIGHT of summer, Irish peasants would celebrate midsummer's eve, which fell during a crucial point of the crop-growing season. Bonfires would be lit all over Ireland and prayers would be said with the hope that crops would grow in healthy abundance. Jumping over the bonfire is a custom that grew out of these celebrations.

Jumping over the flames was thought to bring health and long life, and many men would jump fires to purify themselves before marriage. Couples who were about to be married would also hold hands and jump the fire. This was a way for the couples to acknowledge the journey from their old to new life as husband and wife.

The custom of jumping the fire can be re-created during the later evening part of the reception, once the sun has gone down. If building a fire is not convenient, the bridal couple can ceremoniously jump over a lantern or candle flame. This would symbolically represent the couple jumping into their new life. If using a candle, be sure to use a covered lantern, so there is no chance of the bride's skirts touching the flame. Jumping the fire would be a terrific climax to an authentic *ceili* celebration.

# Chapter Five

# FROM THIS DAY
# FORWARD

Irish Customs from Honeymoon
to Married Life

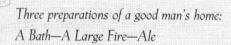

*Three preparations of a good man's home:*
*A Bath—A Large Fire—Ale*

CELEBRATING THE CUSTOMS AND TRADI-
TIONS of Ireland does not have to end for a newly married
couple when the reception is over. There are many ways a
couple can incorporate Irish customs into their daily existence.

This chapter will include ideas for living a life filled with
Irish spirit. There are Irish beliefs that a couple can follow
from the moment they leave the ceremony. There are Irish

superstitions they can heed, which might help them on their daily journey through the world. There are also many simple gifts that a couple can give to each other, to remind them of the joy of their wedding day.

This chapter will offer some words of advice for newly married couples and words of wisdom from the greatest writers and poets in Ireland.

## The Path Home

IT WAS CUSTOMARY in the late eighteenth and early nineteenth centuries for a couple coming home from their wedding festivities to take a different road or path from the one they took to the wedding.

Great pranks were often played on the bride and groom, so this was one way to avoid them. There are also many superstitions regarding a bride being whisked away by Irish fairies for her fine dress. Changing paths was a way to fool the little people.

There is also the belief that a bride and groom are forging a new path together and hence should go down a new road together—still an excellent reason for couples to practice this custom today.

# The Irish Honeymoon

TAKING A HONEYMOON trip was not a common practice in rural Ireland. A trip off Irish soil was considered a lavish expense for most Irish until fairly recently; the rare rural couple might spend a few days after their wedding in a larger city like Dublin or Galway. The Irish were much more apt to have a wedding celebration that went on for one or more days and included the entire community, and then return to the important work of farming and setting up a household immediately after.

Since there are not many Irish customs with regards to a honeymoon, a couple may want to plan a trip to Ireland instead. Honeymooning in Ireland is an excellent way for couples to explore their Irish heritage firsthand. Ireland is one of the most romantic places on earth and an unforgettable trip can be planned that is lavish or very economical, depending on the honeymoon budget.

When planning a trip to Ireland, couples should begin by querying family and friends who have traveled there before visiting a travel agent. Most people who have vacationed in Ireland have favorite places and fantastic stories that they love to share.

# *Dragging Home*

THERE IS A modern custom in Ireland that has survived in updated form from Ireland's past. Today groups of friends will plan to meet a couple at the airport or train station when they are arriving home from their honeymoon.

This is known as "dragging home" the bride and groom and is derived from the old custom whereby, using a jaunting cart, peasants would drag the bridal couple home from their wedding, taking the place of the couple's horses.

A surprise "dragging home" party could be thrown for the newlywed couple on the night of their return from the honeymoon. This will give the couple one last night to bask in attention before settling into their married life and give them a chance to reminisce about their wedding day with friends. Be sure to have candid photos that were taken during the wedding and reception on hand. These will most likely be the first pictures the couple has seen of their wedding and their first chance to relive their special day.

# Salt, Broom, and
# Holy Water

IT IS STILL believed in parts of Ireland that no one should enter their new home without salt, a broom, and holy water. There are many different interpretations of why these three things are most important in a new household.

Salt has always been associated with keeping away evil spirits. (This is why salt is thrown over the shoulder when spilled on a table.) Brooms have been a symbol of domesticity for centuries. It is also thought that all future sadness that might come into the house can be swept away with a daily swish of the broom. Holy water is kept in an Irish house as a daily reminder of a family's faith in God.

A new bride should carry these items across the threshold as she enters her home for the first time—preferably in the arms of her new husband. Carrying the bride over the threshold is another superstition that is commonly practiced in Ireland. This is to trick the Irish little people, who are thought to be lying in wait, ready to spirit a new bride away. In the arms of her new protector, a bride need not fear the *Sidhe*.

# The Hearth Fire

THERE IS A Celtic belief that when a fire is lit and burned for three straight days, the home and land upon which the fire burns will become one with the people who light the flame.

According to Crystal R. Miller, in her article "Lighting the Gods," this fire is called the "needfire" and comes from the Irish term *delan-dhe*, which is the brightness or lighting of the Gods. It is believed in Ireland that every hearth is lit from one central fire, which originally came from the needfire of the Gods.

To practice this custom, a couple can light a candle—perhaps one from their wedding celebration—when they enter their home together for the first time as husband and wife. This candle will hold all the positive, loving feelings from their special day. It is advisable to leave the lit candle in a bathtub or shower when leaving the house so that there is no chance of a fire. A very large or special, slow-burning candle is needed if it is to last for the entire three days.

# Blessing for a New Home

HERE IS A blessing to recite when entering or to post at the door of a couple's new home.

*May God Bless this home*
*All who live here*
*And all who visit here.*
*May your home be filled*
*With God's love and the love*
*You share with one another.*

*May peace, harmony, and laughter*
*Be yours in abundance*
*As long as you live.*

*May you have all the happiness*
*Your Irish heart can hold.*

*May the angels and saints*
*Watch over the newborn,*
*The growing sons and tender daughters,*
*And all your kith and kin.*

*May your home tend the sick,*
*Rest the weary, comfort the dying,*
*Calm the suffering, pity the afflicted,*
*Protect the joyous ones.*

*May God Bless your home*
*With His presence*
*Until you reach your final home—Heaven.*

—SISTER MARY RUTH MURPHY

# The Flowers of Home

AT THE BEGINNING of the twentieth century it was a common custom for the flowers from an Irish bride's wedding bouquet to become the official flowers of her household. When entertaining, a bowl or vase of the bride's signature flowers was always the centerpiece of her table.

This custom is a charming one to practice today. The flowers of the bride's bouquet, and even the groom's boutonniere, when used in floral arrangements will be a constant reminder of a couple's wedding day. A couple may also want to save a vase from their reception tables and leave it in a special place in their home, to be filled often with a couple's signature flowers.

It would also be nice to add a few sprigs of rosemary when creating a signature arrangement, as rosemary is symbolic of remembrance.

# Irish Crystal, Linen, and China

ONE WAY A couple can continue to honor their Irish heritage after the wedding is to register for Irish crystal, linen, and china as wedding gifts. There is a great tradition of using Irish house-wares in homes all around the world. A few pieces of fine Irish crystal and linen were often the only things of value emigrants took with them when they left Irish soil to start a new life in America, Canada, or Australia.

Crystal has been made by the Waterford company for over a hundred years, and they are the most popular maker of Irish crystal. There are also many beautiful designs by Galway, Kinsale, Tyrone, and Tipperary Crystal, all hand-blown and hand-cut by master craftsmen.

Belleek is the oldest china company in Ireland. Since 1847 when John Caldwell Bloomfield started the company on the banks of the River Erne, Belleek has created individual, distinct pieces of parian china, using techniques handed down through generations. No two pieces of Belleek are the same, and it is widely held in Ireland that every newly married couple should be given a "bit of Belleek" to start off their marriage.

Royal Tara is another very popular china company and is based in Galway. They make many different designs of elegant giftware, including full sets of fine china for dining. Recently the Waterford company has begun to design fine china. They have produced a *Book of Kells* pattern based on a Celtic knot design from the original *Kells* manuscript.

Irish linen is considered the finest linen in the world. The technique of making linen was introduced to Ireland in early Christian times, and St. Patrick is said to be buried in a shroud of Irish linen. The Irish linen industry is concentrated in Northern Ireland, between the rivers Bann and Lagan. The river water gives this luxurious linen its unique softness. Making linen is an art, and the finest spinners and weavers in the world are found in the Irish linen community.

Linen is a distinct and sturdy fabric that is said to get better with use. Linen table coverings, sheets, and dish towels for the home can be found from Irish manufacturers like Ferguson, Ewart Liddel, and Blacker's Mill. It is even possible to have pieces of Irish linen embellished with a family crest or monogram.

Owning Irish crystal, linen, and china will remind a couple of their heritage and their wedding day each time it is put to use.

# The Irish Recipe Box

PASSING ON RECIPES from one generation to the next is common practice for Irish women. Many of Ireland's best-loved recipes, those that are distinctly Irish, have survived because mothers sent their daughters to their new homes with a box filled with family recipes.

A newly married woman may want to have a recipe party, inviting her favorite cooks to come and bring their best recipes. Guests may also be asked to bring along the dish, so that the newly married bride will find out firsthand how the dish tastes.

A special notebook or binder should be on hand during the party to collect the recipes and, most importantly, the stories behind the recipes. This will make for a lovely book of cherished memories of times with family and friends, as well as an excellent collection of ideas for good food.

# An Irish Sunday

ONCE THE WEDDING is over and a newly married couple returns to the responsibilities of their everyday life, it is often hard to find time to spend with each other. Take the lead from the Irish and spend a Sunday on "Irish time," which can be defined as moving at a slower pace and having a relaxed constitution.

Start the day off with an Irish breakfast, a filling meal that includes Irish bacon, black and white puddings (a type of spiced sausage), fried or scrambled eggs, grilled tomatoes, grilled mushrooms, and a selection of Irish breads and scones.

After this meal it may be possible to make it over to the couch, where a couple can spend the day reading the great Irish poets, playwrights, or novelists. A bit of Yeats, Wilde, Joyce, or Shaw read aloud will definitely work up an appetite for a hearty Irish stew or other recipe from your newly acquired family recipe box.

# The Irish Child

THE CHILD A couple creates together will be the most cherished and lasting legacy of their Irish heritage. There are some customs of which a couple can partake that will honor their heritage through their child.

Giving a child an Irish name is perhaps the best way to pass on the Irish legacy. A couple might look back at their own family tree for interesting Irish names or name a child after a great Irish statesman or literary figure or perhaps choose a name from Celtic mythology. Irish naming books that will give a couple ideas for baby names, as well as elaborating the history behind the name, are readily available.

According to Linda May Ballard in her book on marriage in Ireland, *Forgetting Frolic*, there are customs that are followed in Ireland after the birth of a child. A wooden box is often put outside the door to a newborn's room. The first time someone carries the baby from the room, he or she steps up on the box; this way the first step the child takes in the world is up not down. A silver coin is also put into a baby's hand, his or her very first, to ensure a life of wealth.

When a baby is christened, the christening gown may be made from the mother's wedding gown if she had a detachable train. Embroidery from the bridal veil can also be used to embellish the christening gown. The top tier of a couple's wedding cake should be served at the christening, with crumbs sprinkled on the baby's head for good luck and long life.

# Irish Wisdom: Advice for the Newly Married

The true perfection of a man lies not in what a man has, but what he is.   —OSCAR WILDE

To know oneself is the first step to knowing love.

An unselfish act is its own reward.

Take time to love and be loved, it is a privilege of the Gods.   —AN IRISH PRAYER

You'll never plough a field by turning it over in your mind.

Argument is the worst sort of conversation.

   —JONATHAN SWIFT

The older the fiddle, the sweeter the tune.

May the roof above you never fall in and may the friends below never fall out.

*May you strive for the health of the salmon, a long life, a full heart, and a wet mouth.*

*Arguments are to be avoided. They are always vulgar and often convincing.* —OSCAR WILDE

*The Golden Rule is that there are no golden rules.*
—GEORGE BERNARD SHAW

A final word of advice to the newly married . . .

*May you live all the days of your life.*
—JONATHAN SWIFT

THERE ARE MANY RESOURCES AVAILABLE to help you plan an Irish wedding. Printing them all here would be next to impossible, and many of the phone numbers and addresses would quickly become outdated. I have created an *Irish Wedding Traditions* website to list the most current and up-to-date resources available. Please visit the site at: www.irishweddingtraditions.com

This website is free and was created as a companion to the book. Enjoy!

*Select
Bibliography*

Adam, David. *The Eye of the Eagle*. London: Society for Promoting Christian Knowlege, 1990.

Baird, Duncan, ed. *Heroes of the Dawn: Celtic Myths*. New York: Time-Life Books, 1996.

Ballard, Linda May. *Forgetting Frolic: Marriage Traditions in Ireland*. Belfast: The Institute of Irish Studies and Folklore Society, 1998.

———. *Tying the Knot: Marriage Traditions in the North of Ireland*. Belfast: The Ulster Folk and Transport Museum, date unknown.

Buckley, Maria. *Irish Marriage Customs*. Cork: Mercier Press, 2000.

Carson, Ciaran. *Irish Traditional Music*. Belfast: The Appletree Press Ltd., 1986.

Cosgrove, Art. *Marriage in Ireland*. Dublin, 1985.

Danaher, Kevin. *In Ireland Long Ago*. Dublin: Mercier Press, 1964.

———. *The Year in Ireland: Irish Calendar Customs*. Cork: Mercier Press, 1972.

Delaney, Mary Murray. *Of Irish Ways*. Minneapolis, Minn.: Dillon Press, 1973.

Dunley, Maired, curator. *The Way We Wore: 250 Years of Irish Clothing and Jewelry*. Dublin: The National Museum of Dublin, 2000.

Foster, R. F., ed. *Oxford Illustrated History of Ireland*. New York: Oxford University Press, 1989.

Hall, Mr. and Mrs. S. C. *Ireland, Its Scenery, Character etc.* 3 vols. London, 1845.

Johnson, Margaret M. *Irish Heritage Cookbook*. San Francisco: Chronicle Books, 1999.

Joyce, P. W. *A Social History of Ancient Ireland*. Dublin: M. H. Gill & Son, 1908.

*The Little Book of Irish Wisdom*. New York: Double Day Direct, 1992.

Llywelyn, Morgan. *Finn MacCool*. New York: Tor Books, 1995.

Longfeld, Ada. *Irish Lace*. Dublin: Eason Publishing Company, 1978.

Loughney, Martin. *Springs of Irish Love*. Dublin: Infinity Books, 1991.

*The Matchmaker*. Mark Joffe, director. 1997. Polygram Filmed Entertainment.

Murphy, Michael J. *At Slieve Gullion's Foot*. Dundalk, 1940.

———. *Sayings and Stories from Slieve Gullion*. Dundalk, 1990.

ni Dhoireann, Kym. "Irish Fire Festivals." *Think!* vol. 2 (Spring/Beltaine 1997).

O'Donohue, John. *Anam Cara: Spiritual Wisdom from the Celtic World.* London: Bantam Press, 1997.

O'Farrell, Padraic. *Superstitions of the Irish Country People.* Cork: Mercier Press, 1978.

O'Sullivan, Paul, ed. *Field and Shore: Daily Life and Traditions, Aran Islands, 1900.* Dublin: O'Brien Educational Ltd., 1977.

Power, Patrick C. *Sex and Marriage in Ancient Ireland.* Dublin: Mercier Press, 1997.

Tegy, W. *The Knot Tied.* London, 1877.

Thomas Dillon's Claddagh Museum Brochure. Galway, 1998.

White, Carol. *The History of Irish Fairies.* Cork: Mercier Press, 1976.

Wilde, Lady. *Irish Cures, Mystic Charms and Superstitions.* New York: Sterling Publishing Co., 1991.

About.com. *Wedding Blessings*, Racheal Shreckengast
  *www.weddings.about.com*
About Ireland
  *www.Ireland-Information.com*
Aon Celtic Art and Illumination. *Art History of the Celtic Cross*,
  Cari Burke
  *www.aon-celtic.com*
*Archaeology in Ireland: The Celtic High Cross*, Mike Carson
  *www2.hawaii.edu/mcarson/*
The Brian Bank
  *www.cftech.com/BrianBank*

Celtic Connection. *Celtic Wedding Traditions for Modern Lovers,*
  C. Austin
  *www.celtic-connection.com*
Clover Specialty Company
  *www.fourleafclover.com*
Coat of Arms
  *www.coatsofarms.addr.com*
Flockharts of Edinburgh
  *www.Flockharts.com*
FoodIreland.com
  *www.Irishfood.com*
*Gaelic Harps and Harpers in Ireland and Scotland,* Robert Ruadh
  *www.silcom.com*
Guinness Brewery
  *http://www.ivo.se/guinness*
Heart of Imladris. *The Legend of the Claddagh*
  *http://member.aol.com/imladriscb/index.htm*
The Heraldica Organization
  *www.heraldica.org*
The House Shadow Drake Oynx. *Celtic Herbs* and *Lighting the
  Gods,* Crystal R. Miller
  *www.witchhaven.com/shadowdrake*
International Colored Gemstone Association
  *www.gemstone.org*
Ireland for Visitors. *Winning the Turf: Fuel for the Family*
  *www.goireland.about.com*
St. Brigid's Shrine Page
  *http://www.npi.ie/~mgordon/st_brigid.html*
Trade Shop
  *www.tradeshop.com*

Turlough O'Carolan
   *www.contemplator.com*
University of Galway
   *http://seaweed.ucg.ie/botany/default.html*
Webtender. *Mixed drink recipes*
   *www.webtender.com*
Wedding Guide U.K.
   *www.weddingguide.co.uk*
Weddings On Line. *Ask the Experts*, Kim McGuire
   *www.weddingsonline.ie*

*Notes*

*Notes*